Swimming my way through the depths of depression

Madame Phoenix

(Laura Jayne Inglis)

Cataloguing-in-Publication entry is available from the National Library of Australia:
www.catalogue.nla.gov.au

Title: Swimming My Way through the Depths of Depression
Author: Madame Phoenix (Laura Jayne Inglis)
ISBN: 978-0-6459251-0-4

Cover design by Odyssey Publishing (www.odysseypublishing.com)
All artwork by Madame Phoenix (Laura Jayne Inglis) unless otherwise credited

THIS BOOK IS DEDICATED TO MY FAMILY AND FRIENDS,
WHO STOOD STILL WITH ME WHEN I NEEDED IT MOST.

AND TO MY FUNCTIONAL NEUROLOGICAL DISORDER
(FND) FAMILY AND ALL OTHER SURVIVORS OF THIS
DEBILITATING DISABILITY:
STAY STRONG. WE'VE GOT THIS.

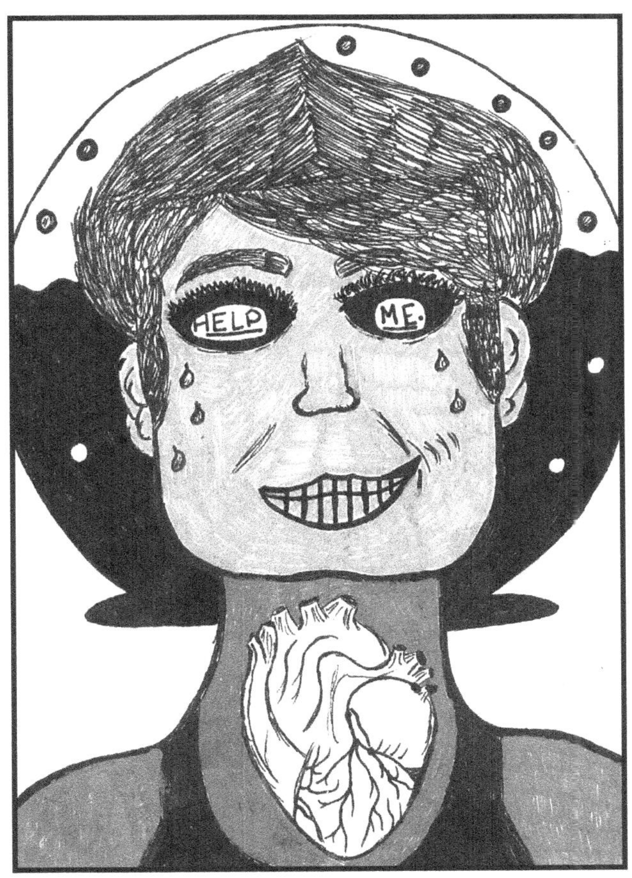

The reality of living with FND

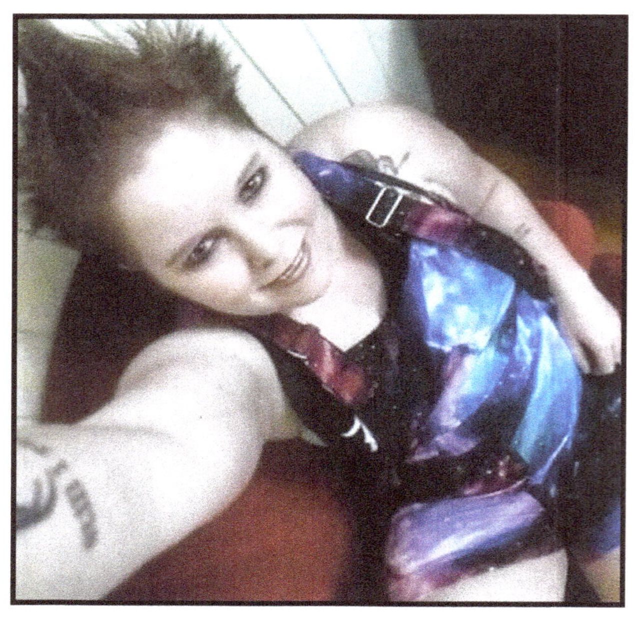

Madame Phoenix Laura Jayne Inglis:
Artist. Poet. Storyteller. Visionary. Writer.

An unstoppable force of nature.

You've seen my descent; now watch my uprising.

CONTENTS

INTRODUCTION

From an early age, I learnt the immense influence and capacity in literature and how words had the ability to empower and cause tremendous healing as well as the potential to cause great harm to one another. Since the of seven, I have celved into the magical world of literature, and would often write poems and have them pinned to my local swimming club noticeboard. My show-and-tells in primary school usually consisted of me reciting love poetry to whom I believed were my young betrothed. Except, of course, for that one time when I belted out the "Glory of Love" to my true love in Grade 1 (Ah, nothing like your first love, am I right?).

Writing, for me, is like making music. It is playing the music of my heart, articulating my heartache, using lyrics, melodies, and rhythms to encapsulate my journey, pain, loneliness, love, joys, and hopes of my very being. It is also about being my utmost vulnerable self. When I write, I am exposing my deepest secrets. I am baring myself for all the world to see. I hold nothing back.

It has helped me cope with many struggles, including my diagnosis of Functional Neurological Disorder (FND) and living with Post Traumatic Stress Disorder and Major Depressive Disorder. In 2019, I was involved in a car accident that caused a serious head injury and ultimately resulted in the diagnosis of FND. In a few short months, my life changed drastically, and I seemed to lose everything that mattered to me: my career working with children, my license and independence, and the ability to walk, talk, and eat normally. It was extremely debilitating and took months of intense rehabilitation to recover.

During this time, I was unable to skate, which was something I was passionate about. I would often skate up to sixteen hours a week and was also involved with a local Roller Derby league. To cope with this loss, I decided to pick up a pencil and draw. I'd never been any good at drawing; nevertheless, I drew two feet and wrote a poem, and from there, a beautiful habit grew. I found an incredible release for my depression—one that led to hundreds of sketches, poems, and paintings, and various creative enterprises.

It has taken me great courage to learn to share my words with the world, but I believe art is to be celebrated and experienced by the masses rather than the minority. It is my hope that my book may bring comfort and peace to the weary, even if it's just one person. I wish you joy in reading my magical writings, and may it be as wonderful for you as it was for me bringing it together.

Madame Phoenix

PART I

Drowning

I struggled under the weight of all the hardship and pressure.
Everything I held dear was disappearing.
Slipping from my fingers and vanishing, never to be seen aga n, like
sunken treasure.

– Exert

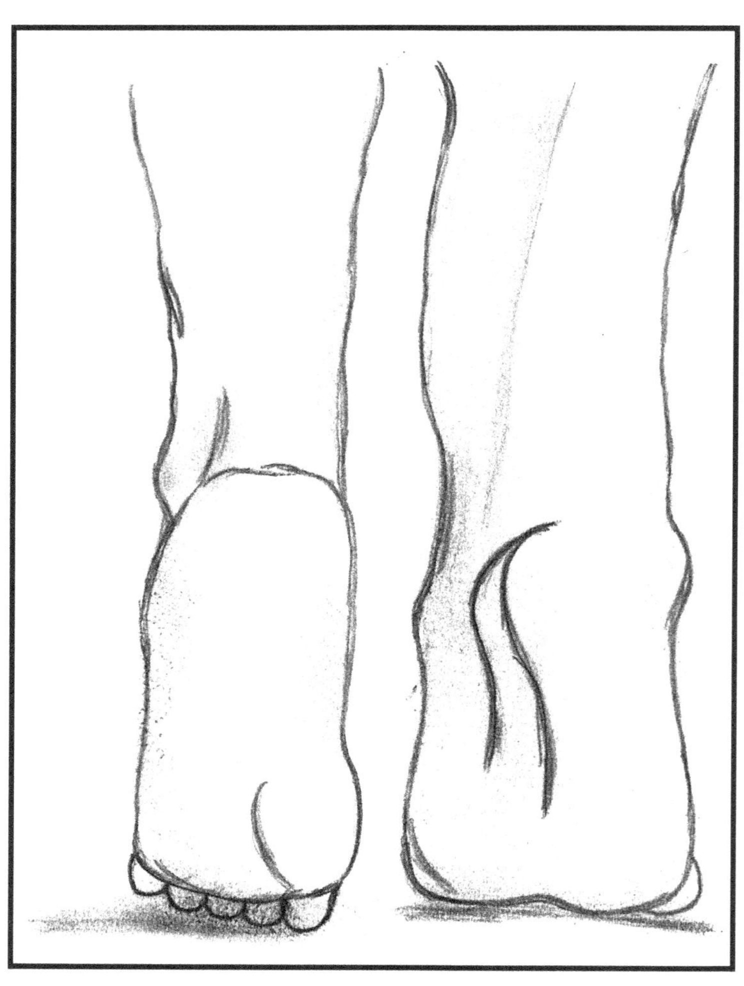

Walk with Me

WALK WITH ME

Walk with me
A thousand miles
A thousand tales
Only then you'll see
the story that is me.

Each tale intricately woven
Overlapping at every beginning
and at every ending.
This is me.
This is me.

Walk with me
Follow my footsteps
One by one
Then you will learn
the beat of my heart.

Every tale intricately woven
Overlapping at every beginning
and at every ending.
This is me.
This is me.

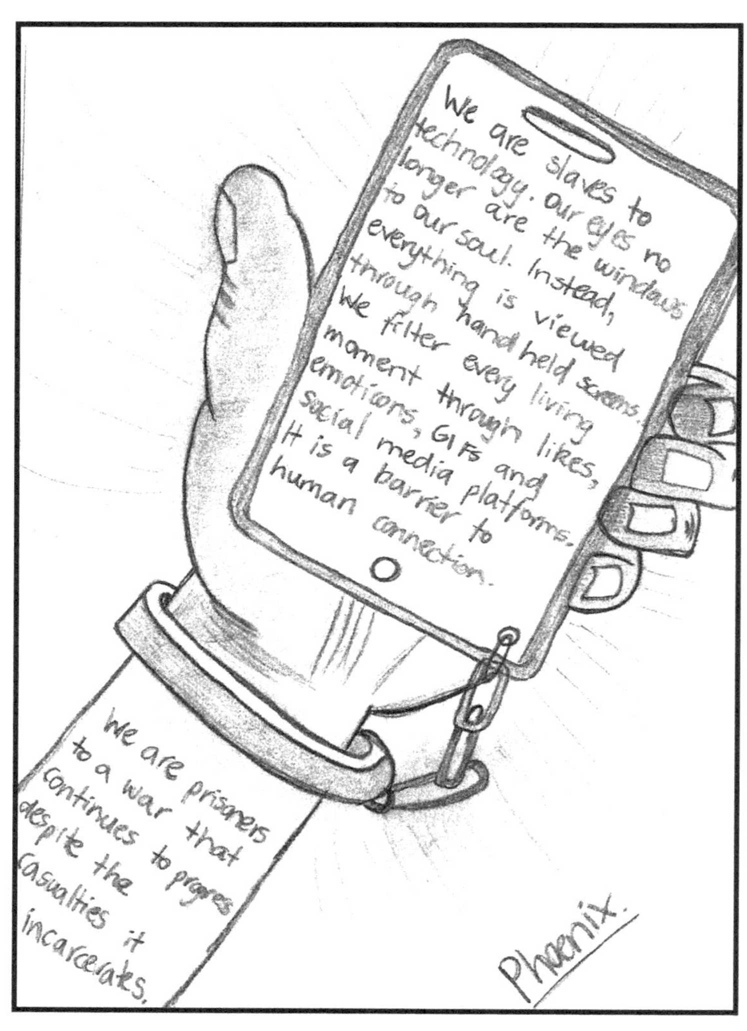

Prisoners of Society

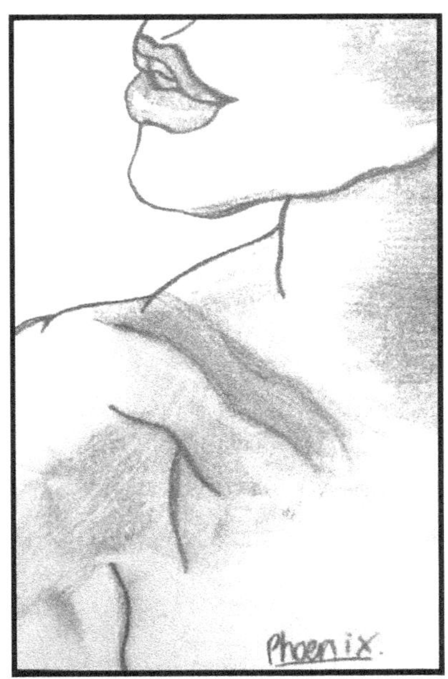

Still I Rise

COME CLOSER

"Come closer," she whispered,
"and look at how I move. What do you see?"
I laughed and replied, "You seem active and healthy,
like a child, running through the woods, wild and free."

"Come closer," she whispered,
"and listen to my words. What do you hear?"
I smiled and said, "Happiness and joy, not a care in the world. Surely you have no burdens to bear?"

"Come closer," she whispered,
"and look into my face. What do you see?"
"Oh, that's easy," I replied, "I see your smile, wider than the ocean. You look happy to me."

"Come closer," she whispered,
"and look into my eyes. Tell me what you see."

It was then I paused, and I stared, for I could not believe. The sight staring back at me was not at all what I thought it to be.
"Oh no," I cried in shame and empathy.
Then I whispered back to her, this stranger now she seemed...

"Darkness and longing, deeper than the oceans and lower than the valleys.
Pain and suffering, beyond measures man can compare, and, most of all, a tormented soul with so little light to bare."

"Ah," she sighed, "finally...you have seen the depression that consumes and resides within me."

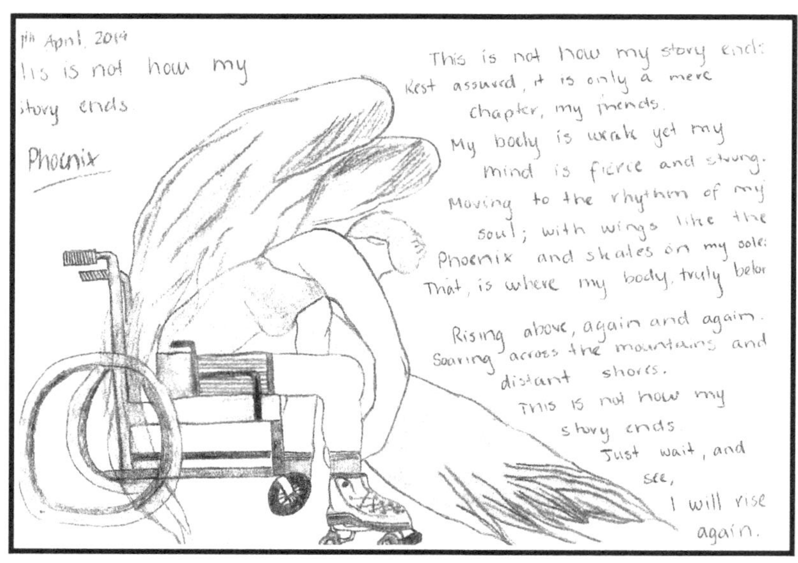

This is not how my story ends

Every day I fight a waging war against my body.
It forces me down deeper and deeper in trenches.
I struggle to breathe, and my thoughts are foggy
From the strain it heaves on me – it is relentless.
I swear, I curse, I scream, I cry.
I endure this madness day and night.
There is no reprieve,
Nor is there a definitive end in sight.
I cannot tell what each day will bestow.
Yet time has taught me, and now I know,
I must fight with everything I possess
In order to survive and conquer, no less.
I didn't choose this battle, you see.
But I'll be damned if I let it defeat me.

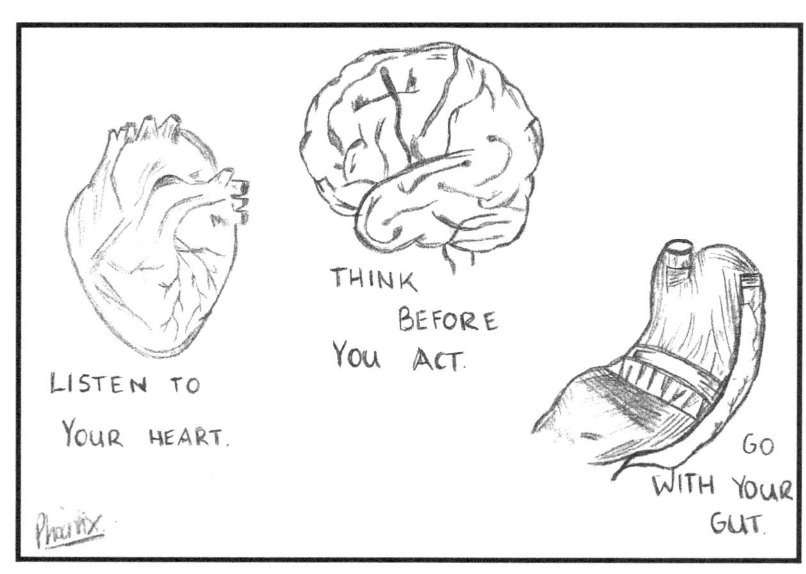

Instincts

GRIEVING

Lately I find myself holding my hands to my womb,
Caressing the space where he or she may have taken up room.
Alas, I was cursed with infertility, shattering my childhood dream of motherhood.
Instead, my infertility turned me down a dark and isolated pathway.
One that winds and loops, trails and blazes
through scenery after scenery,
some picturesque, though most dark and twisted,
cruel and cold, always leading me to the infirmary.

I am the main casualty of this path I walk, barefoot and alone.
Though many have tried to help, it is one I must walk on my own.
To seek refuge and contentment in other avenues.
To find somewhere to plant my feet, rest my head, pour my heart, and call my home.

You see, I have all this love to give,
love I'd kept with me as a child.
I nourished and watered it, watched it grow in time,
believing one day I would have a partner and many little ones to love unconditionally,
these children of mine.

But life is wicked, and the world had other plans.
It chose instead to give me a broken womb and an ill-riddled body.
My dreams of having children were ripped away from me.
I could not carry them; my body wouldn't let me.
Though I've known this since I was in my twenties, the pain of this part of my story
still stays with me.

Thus, lately I find myself laying at night with my hands across my womb and the tears falling as I grieve

for the children I don't have and being mum to the many children I dreamed I would give birth to.

And for now, that's okay, it's where I am and that's all I can do.

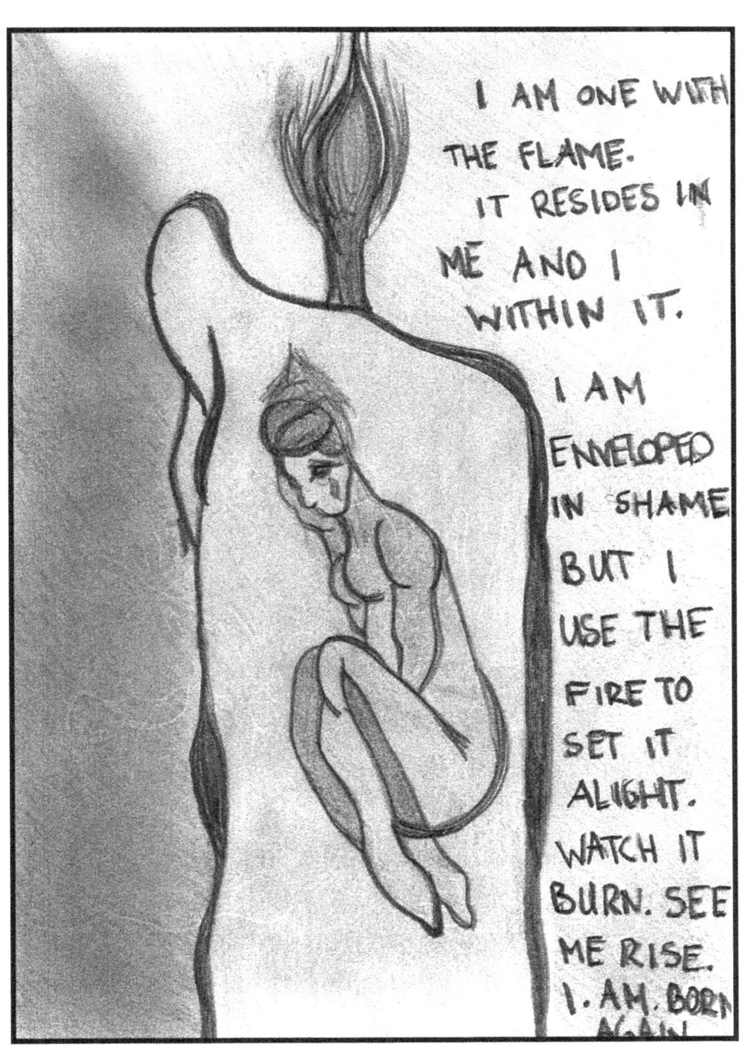

Fire resides within me. I will rise again.

LISTEN. THINK. FEEL.

You are more than the sum of your parts.
You are intricately woven.
There is no one else quite like you.
Listen to your heart; follow your own rhythm.
Dance to the beat of your chambers. Close your eyes and breathe.

LISTEN. THINK. FEEL.

Your neural pathways are etched into every fibre of your being.
The blueprint of your mind and body is like no other.
You are more than the sum of your parts.
You are more than enough.

Darling angel of mine,
Let me caress you in my arms.
Let these tears upon your face,
Flow softly on my skin.

Share with me your pain and sorrow,
Burdened by your heart.
Let me lift your tired spirit,
And carry it through the stars.

Your soul is sad and weary,
Tired from the long journey.
So let me hold it close to mine,
And heal it with my love.

Hold you as I love you so,
With a love that's always true.

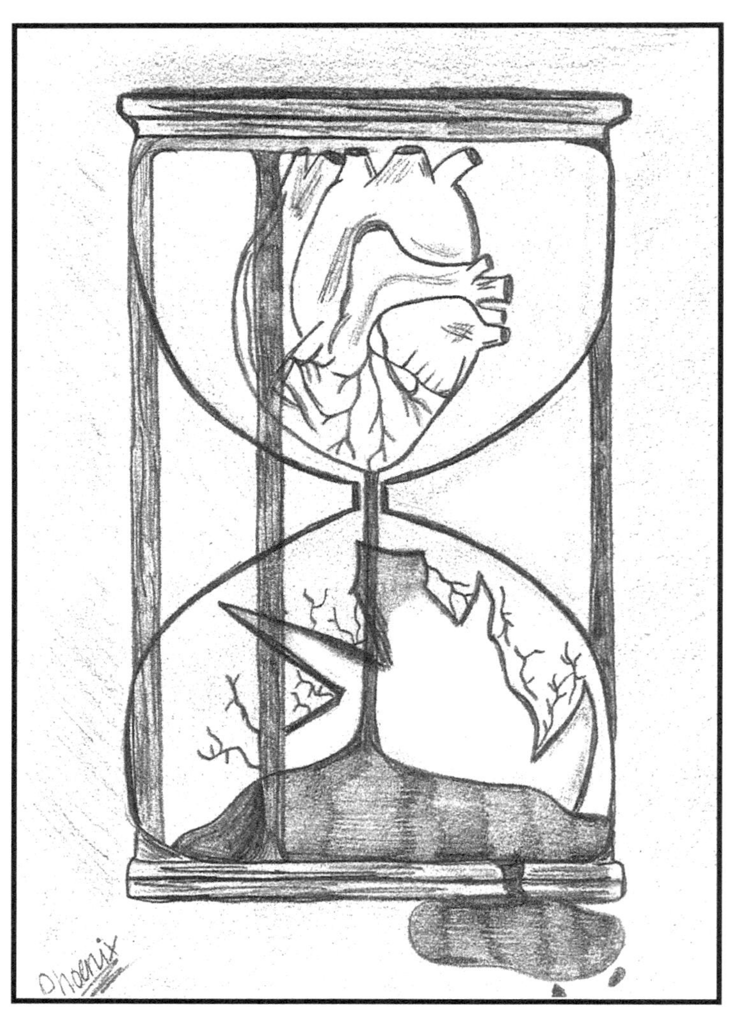

Heart Hourglass

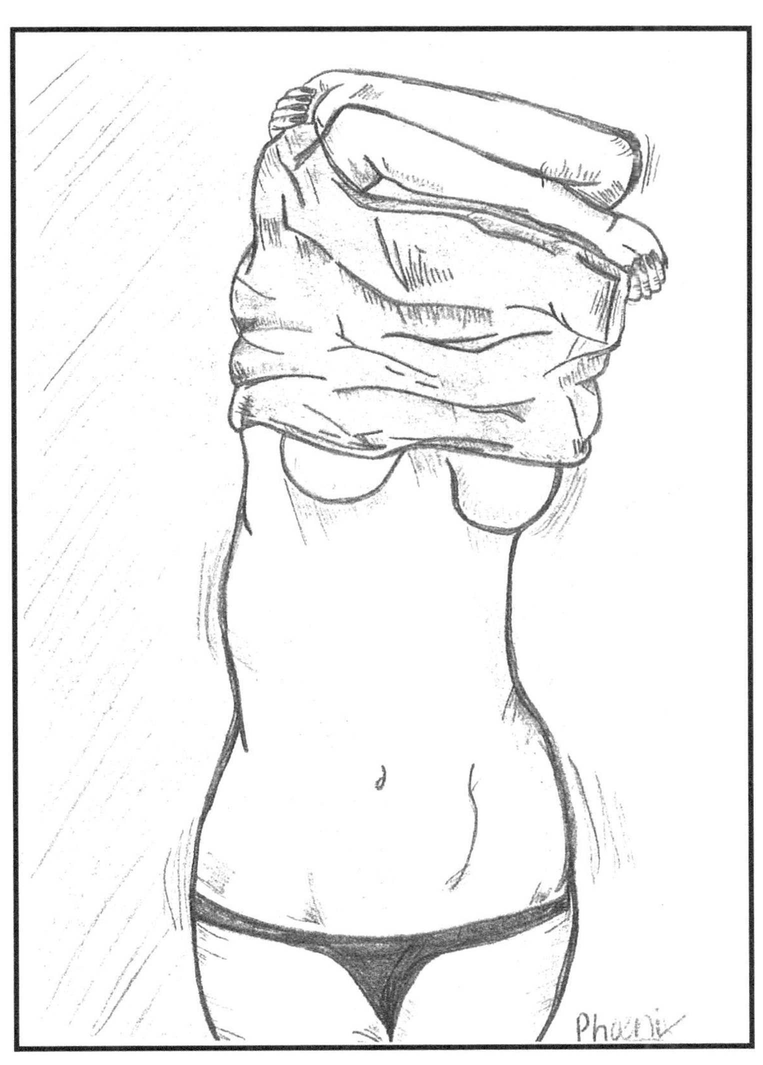

You are Woman. You are Free.

Body image, to me, is not what we look like,
but rather how we feel.
You may look at this picture and cry,
"I look nothing like this woman!"
No one does; it's not real.

Her body is toned and slim, so perfectly formed.
Why draw something that reinforces the 'ideal woman' to which society has con-
formed?

What you're missing is the shape,
the contours of her body and her essence.
Her sturdy thighs, the curves of her hips,
and how her torso stretches as she reaches for the sun's first kiss.

This is how I feel.
This is how we should ALL feel.
Regardless of how we look on the outside.
Let's radiate that which we feel on the inside.

She is a champion, a warrior, a goddess, and fighter. She is somebody's partner,
friend, mother or daughter.
Just like you. Just like me.
She is woman. She is free.

I say to you earnestly, embrace every fibre of your being.
Close your eyes and learn to look beyond the flaws
you've been fooled into seeing.

Take your time, caressing every inch of your frame.
From the tips of your toes to the strands of your hair.
Feel the warmth of your body and let go of the shame.

For you are filled with beauty, soul, power, and grace.
There is no one quite like you.
So please, learn to embrace.

The you that you are, in all its entity.
Let go of what you look like and instead
Own how you feel as well as your identity.

You are woman. You are free.
You are everything you think and feel, trust me. Believe.

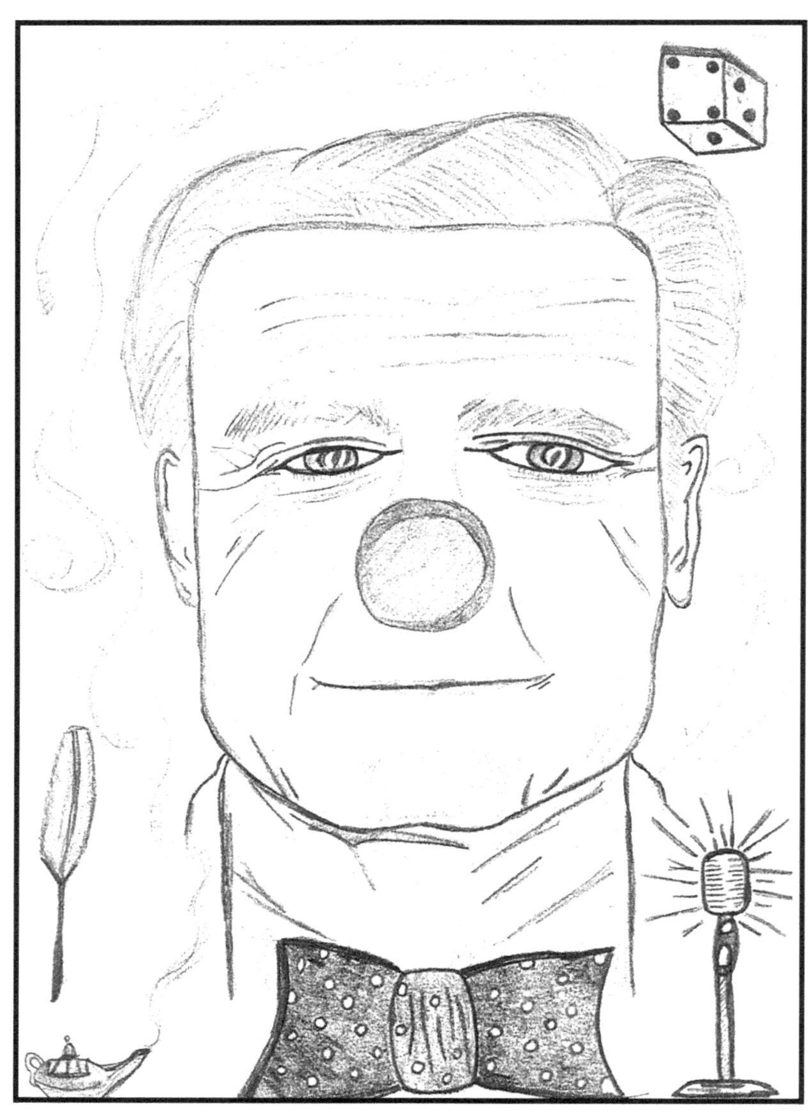

Robin Williams in all his glory

There is too much noise

Yet it is oh, so, quiet.

Fill the damn silence.

Wake up the neighborhood.

Masquerade – turn your faces from the world.

I am empty. I am full. I am here. No one sees me.

Masquerade.

Take the damn pills.

"You'll feel better," they said.

"Do the therapy.

Stick to the plan. It will be okay."

Or so they say.

Masquerade – turn your faces from the world.

I am empty. I am full. I am here. No one sees me.

Masquerade.

Take the damn pills.

Just breathe. 1, 2, 3, 4, 5, 6, 7. Breathe.

Swallow the tablets.

"You'll feel better," they said.

"You'll be okay," they promised.

THEY PROMISED.

Blank faces everywhere I go.

Emptiness all around,

Resonating amongst the people.

Depression is the latest contagion.

Masquerade – turn your faces from the world.

I am empty. I am full. I am here. No one sees me.

Masquerade.

Take the damn pills.

Dawn breaks, the crow is calling as she slips quietly down the stairs, making her way down to the car through the fog. Her breath blowing puffs of smoke as she fumbled for her keys in the misty morning. "Mercy me! What was I thinking" She muttered to herself, even though she knew full well what the answer to that question: That was precisely the problem; she wasn't thinking. Or maybe she was. Just one thing. Go. Leave. Drive and don't look back. Leaning against her car she continued to fumble for her keys; her blue Mazda with Elvis number plates and bright-blue, leopard print seat covers. The car and all its trimmings were beckoning her through the window; yearning, as she was, to disappear. In hopes, the drive would put some much-needed distance between the depression she faced. A darkness heavy and draining it felt as though she was being smothered. Surely anywhere must be better than here?

Finally, she found the keys and burst through the door like a bull at a gate. She couldn't help but laugh at herself a moment. Remembering a younger version of herself thinking the saying was "Bullet at a gate" and being completely befuddled as to why someone would shoot a gate. Whether it was intentional or if someone simply had terrible aim! The engine purred as she turned the key, almost a grumble at her as though slightly disgruntled at being woken so early. Eventually she came around and warmed up, humming with eagerness for what lay before them. Before they hit the road Maggie searched her glove box for the CD she absolutely needed – Brandi Carlile: The Story – then off she went. Quietly reversing down the driveway to not wake the rest of the family, her parents on the south-western side of the house whilst her brother was in a deep slumber on the other side of their home. Although she was 19 and an adult and could technically do what she wanted, her parents' approval and validation still meant everything to her. Even now as she was making her way towards the highway, she couldn't help but hear her Dad's voice critiquing her every move and criticising this need for, "this senseless and wasteful time of resources". To be fair, there was some truth to it, but she just had to go and get away for the day. She had already called in sick, which was also technically true, as her menstrual cramps could be compared with a drill going full circuit through her uterine wall. Thus, onwards, and upwards she drove. Maggie smiled. She wound down the windows the whole way, blasted the stereo full power to Brandi's No. 1 bestseller, "The Story" for the second time in a row, and took the first exit onto the highway towards Burleigh Heads, the Gold Coast: her home away from home. The cold, misty morning air stung on her face and her voice wavered across the windy highway as she sung to Brandi's lyrics. She could already feel the burden being lifted and her worries being whisked away by the power of singing, art and the promise of the seas: the warm, golden sand sifting through her fingers and toes; the ocean waves crashing, beating to her cardiac rhythm, and vast blue skyline atop the open sea – reminding her that despite the constraints and chains she feels. In truth, she is free. The cell she feels imprisoned in is merely a farce that society and her fears and insecurities have conjured. Which is why she needed to get away for a day, to her home away from home. To remind herself that just like the deep, blue sea; she is free. She is free and she is safe and home.

PART II

Sinking

> I crumbled beneath the weight,
> my body sank to the ocean floor.
> It was empty, dark, and cold.
> I curled into a ball.
> I couldn't take it anymore.

– Exert

The hospital is incredibly quiet. Its hum of noises are smoothly running along like clockwork. My head, on the other hand, is oh so loud. It's like a carnival after hours, where everyone has gone mad and there is no order. Chaos, madness, insanity, anarchy everywhere. I want to scream, but I still have trouble speaking and my face is contorted. It has a mind of its own, twisting and straining in unbelievably awkward ways. It hurts like hell. I feel as though a dozen hands are grappling at the flesh on my face, pulling and stretching in different directions, so tightly I can scarcely blink or breathe. My neck cranes too, jerking back and rolling against my shoulders, mainly my right one. At least when that happens, I can see outside my hospital bedroom window; it's pitch-black with tiny flickering city lights of various colours. They remind me of the fireflies up at the golf course back at Mum and Dad's.

Can I stay in bed all day?
If I do, will it keep the world at bay?
The sounds of traffic and people out on the street
Creates a white noise to accompany my defeat.

There is nothing I'd rather do
Than stay at home, alone with you.
Hold you tenderly against my heart.
Praying desperately that we'll never part.

I'll keep you safe; stay strong and steadfast.
In the good times and bad, through the storms life casts.
We'll be okay, as long as we're together here.
Wrapped between my sheets, so vulnerable, so bare.

I'll say to you what I've always held true.
You are vulnerable and worthy. You are perfect. I love you.
But alas, it seems this cannot be,
For despite all your promises, you have abandoned me.
Gone away, never to be seen again.
Oh how I miss you – my love, my companion, my long lost friend.

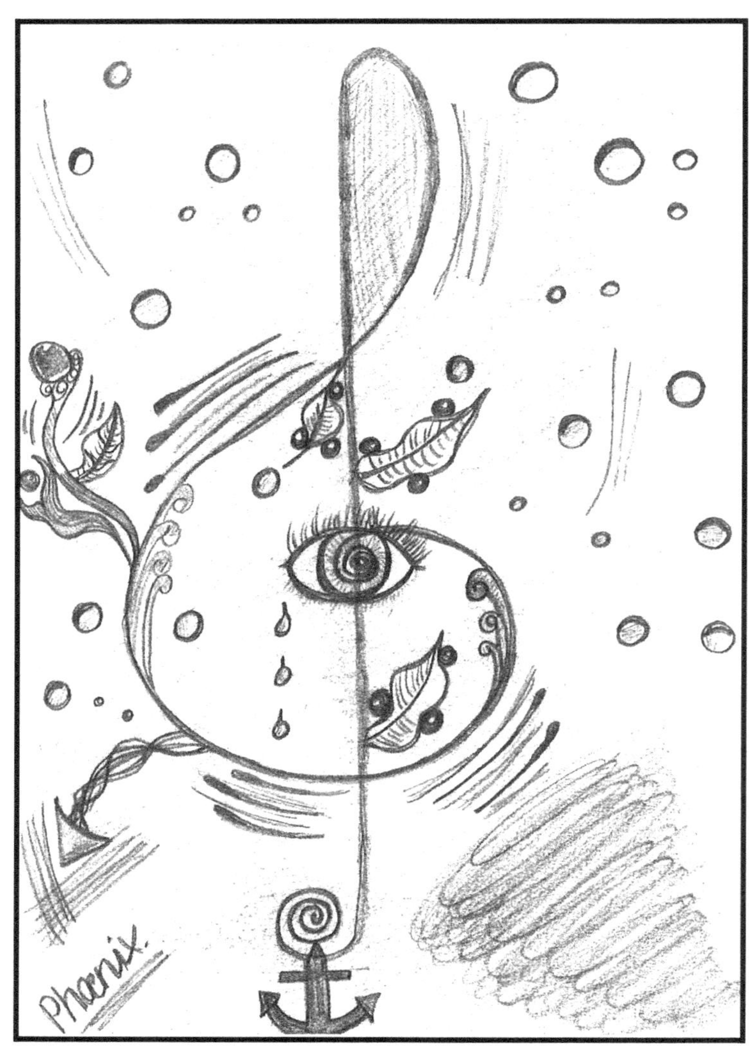

Beauty within us all – Keep breathing

"And I can't help regretting that I never got to tell her how much she was loved," she gasped and cried to me as she finally unearthed the level of her grief.

"I would do anything to wrap my arms around her one last time, to hold her face in my hands and feel her heart beat against mine. Did she know? Did she know how loved and treasured she was? Did I make her feel respected and empowered and worthy? Were my words and actions enough?"

She reached into the darkness with desperation, her anguish her only companion as she searched for answers she longed for but no one could give her, least of all me.

"You did all you could, my love. You did all you could. You loved her as passionately and as deeply as you do everyone in your life, and if that wasn't enough for her to feel seen or heard, then there isn't anything more you could have done. We can't save the ones we love. They have to save themselves. They have to learn they are worth saving and to be their own heroes. You did everything you could in the time you had together, and that's all you know; for now, at least."

"But is this how our story ends? I never thought, never dreamed, that this would be how our story would end. I never...I never had the chance...the chance to say how much I loved her or the chance...the chance...to say goodbye..."

Her voice trailed off as she cried harder and harder, the full extent of her heartache finally reaching capacity, like angry waves crashing against boats at sea. She was at breaking point. There was nothing to do but sit and be still together in this storm, in her chaos.

"Just breathe, my darling. Everything is not okay, but it will be one day, and it's okay that it isn't right now. Just breathe. I'm here. I'm here."

And we sat on the phone together for as long as she needed as she cried and grieved for the love of her life, a best friend and companion she'd shared a life with and a soul she cared deeply for despite all that had happened and all the time had passed. Because she loved fiercely and passionately with no limitations, nor beginning or ending, and I hoped and prayed that this was not how their story ends...

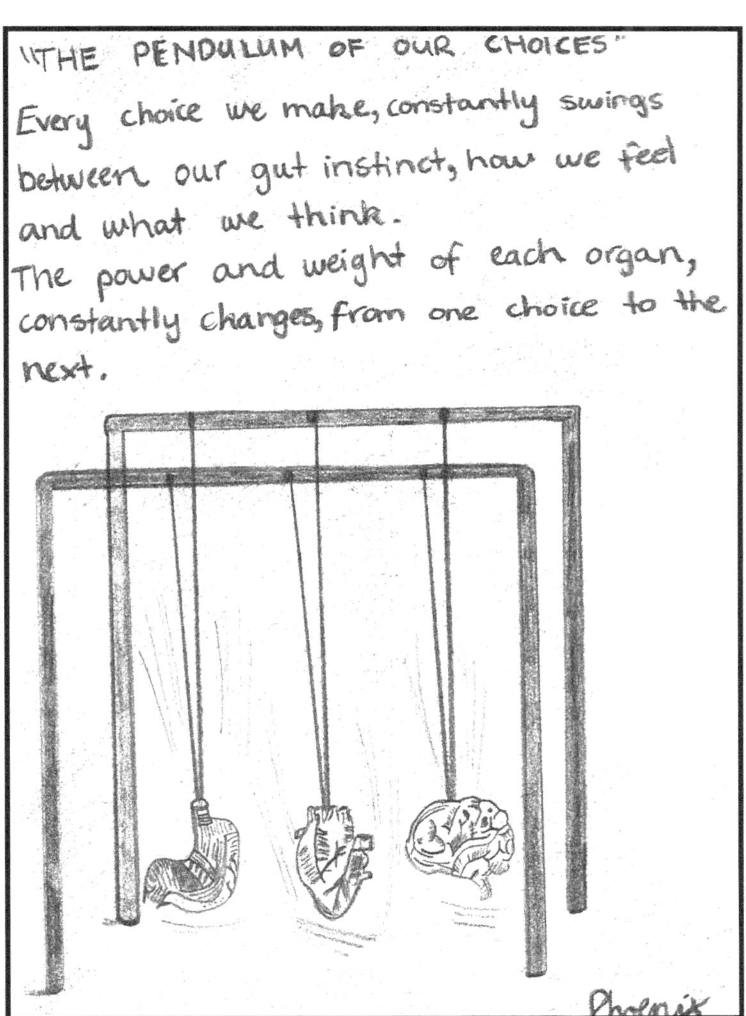

The Pendulum of our choices

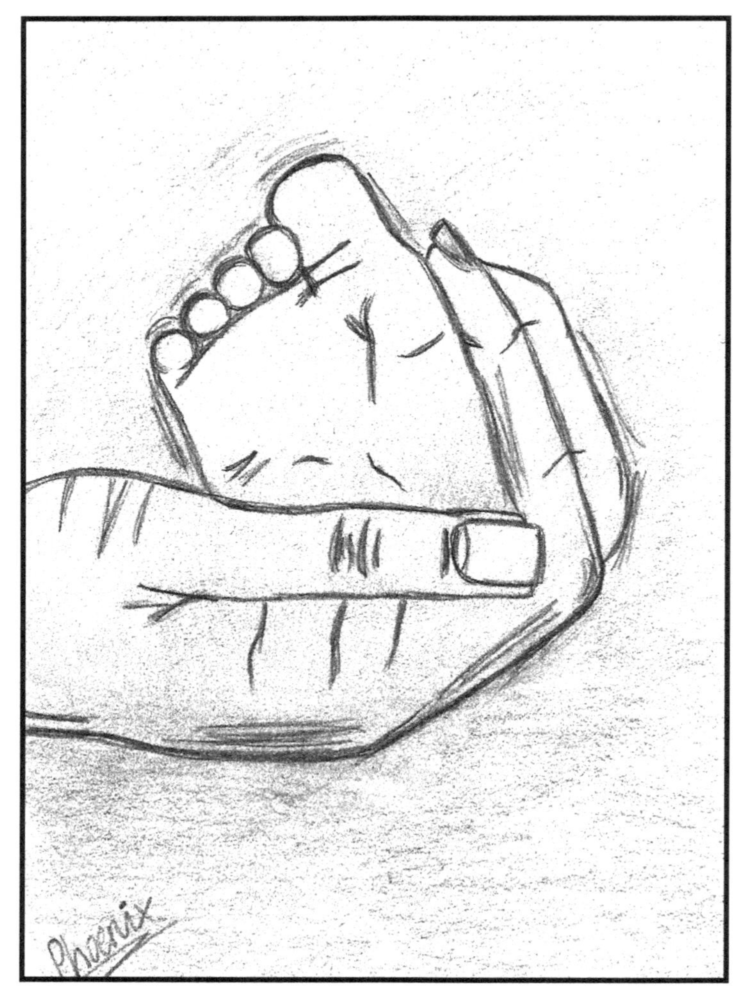

Mumma and Baby

YOU BROUGHT ME TO MY KNEES

But there's no point in me still sitting round
Wondering whether you're coming back to repair what's broken.
Because I can't help but think if you were going to
It would have happened by now.
I guess some wounds are always left open.

You took us through the universe
Across the stars and seas.
You promised me the world
Instead, you brought me to my knees.

But that's what happens when you fall in love with someone
Who has seen the depths of despair and been broken and abused
You're waging a war against the fragmented pieces of their mind.
Do your best, but finally their demons win, leaving you broken and confused.
Yet despite the sorrow, I'd do it all over, just to be with you again.
To hold you close, hear you laugh, touch your face and dance until dawn.
You were worth it, every moment. I still love you and always will.
So, you can go
I'll move on, but know this – I'm standing still for you.
Always have, always will.

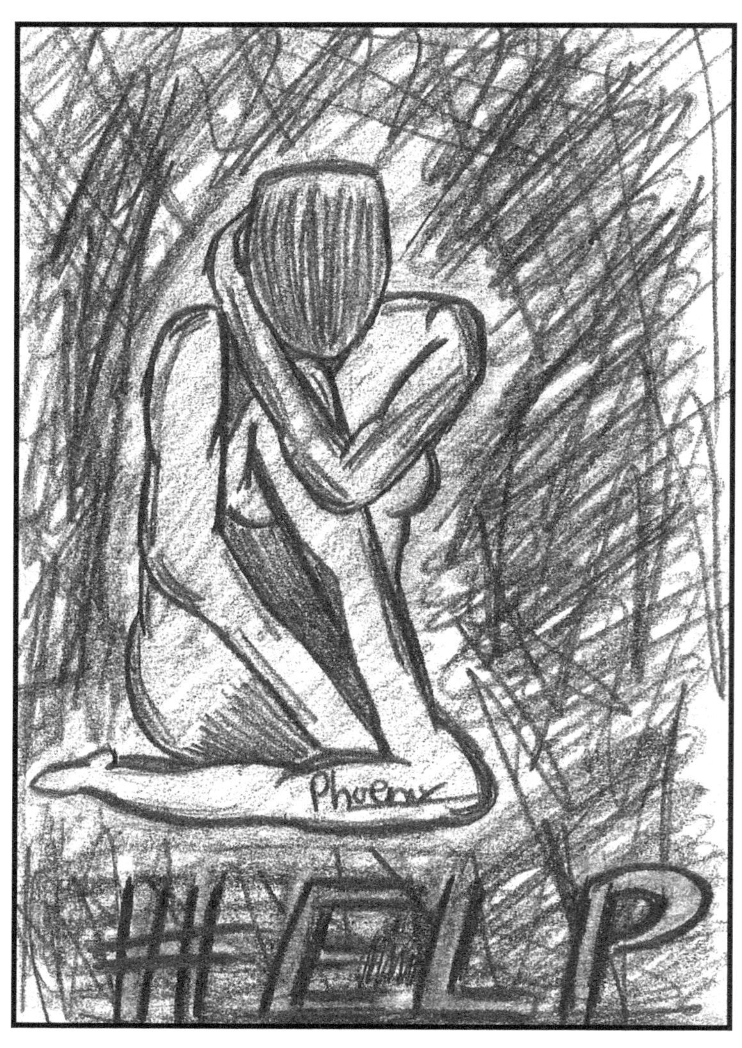

I am wrapped in shame

I am wrapped in shame.
It envelopes me.
Casting a shadow on everything I touch
For all the world to see.

I am wrapped in shame.
It engulfs me.
Suffocating me while I sleep.
Every breath I take
Heavy with agony.

I am wrapped in shame.
It swallows me.
Taunting me as I walk.
Echoing my fears at every turn.
See how the shadows dance at my feet?

I am wrapped in shame.
It consumes me.
Drowning out all the light
That once resided in me.

I am wrapped in shame.
It is a part of me,
One I cannot escape
No matter how desperately I flee.

I am wrapped in shame.
I cannot break free.
You see
The shame that I have carried for so long
Is now all that's left of me.

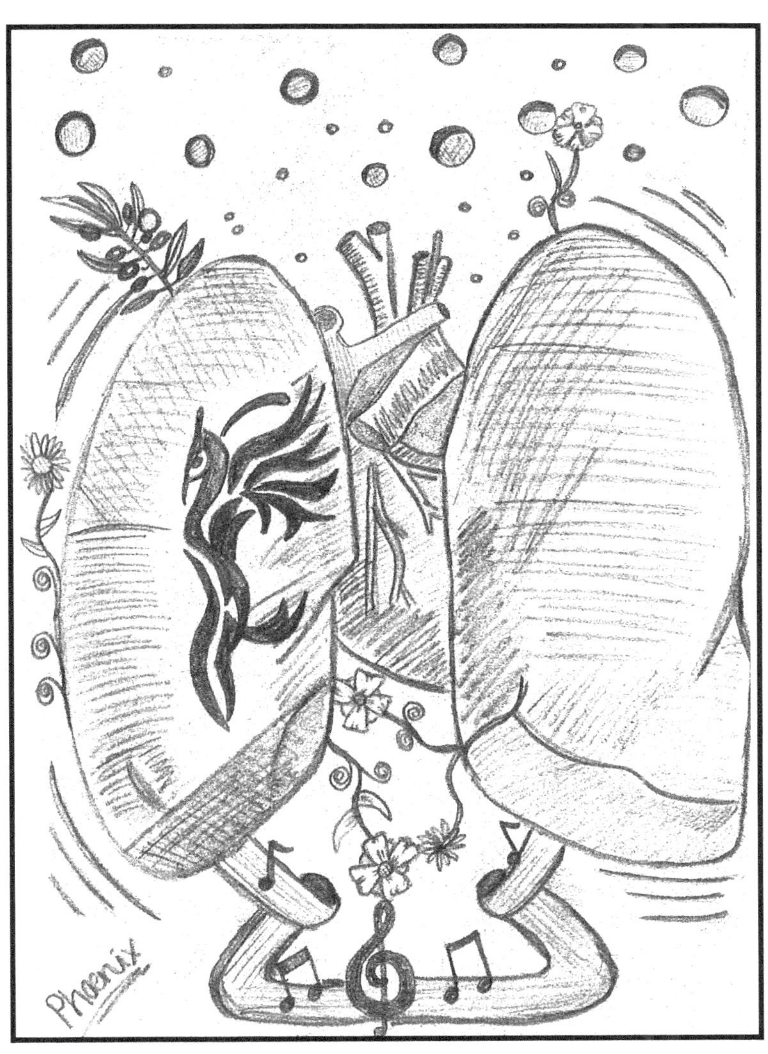

Remember all the things you love, and breathe.

HIS LIGHT BEYOND THE

DARKNESS

Darkness calls out to me,
Walls are caving in,
Shadows cause the light to flee,
I'm slowly suffocating.

I hear the voices calling me,
Muffled though they sound,
Of friends, colleagues, family.
I am not easily found.

I'm sinking in the depths of the sea,
Treading water, while all around me others swim.
Oh, how hard it is to breathe.
How much longer can I last before I truly give in?

The coldness numbs the years of hurt,
While the ocean pulls me deeper still.
My lungs, my heart, and my head – they burst.
Surely, this is not God's will?

"No, my child," He gently whispers, beckoning me to stay.
"I have so many plans for you, to prosper, thrive, and bloom.
Trust in me, have faith, hold on, and listen when I say:
This pain you feel, though it aches, I promise will end soon.

So reach out to me, take my hand, you've nothing left to fear.
I'll hold you close, I'll keep you safe, and of that I can be sure.
Don't look back, turn your gaze to me, I promise you I'm here.
Rest my child, I am your refuge. I'll be your light, forevermore."

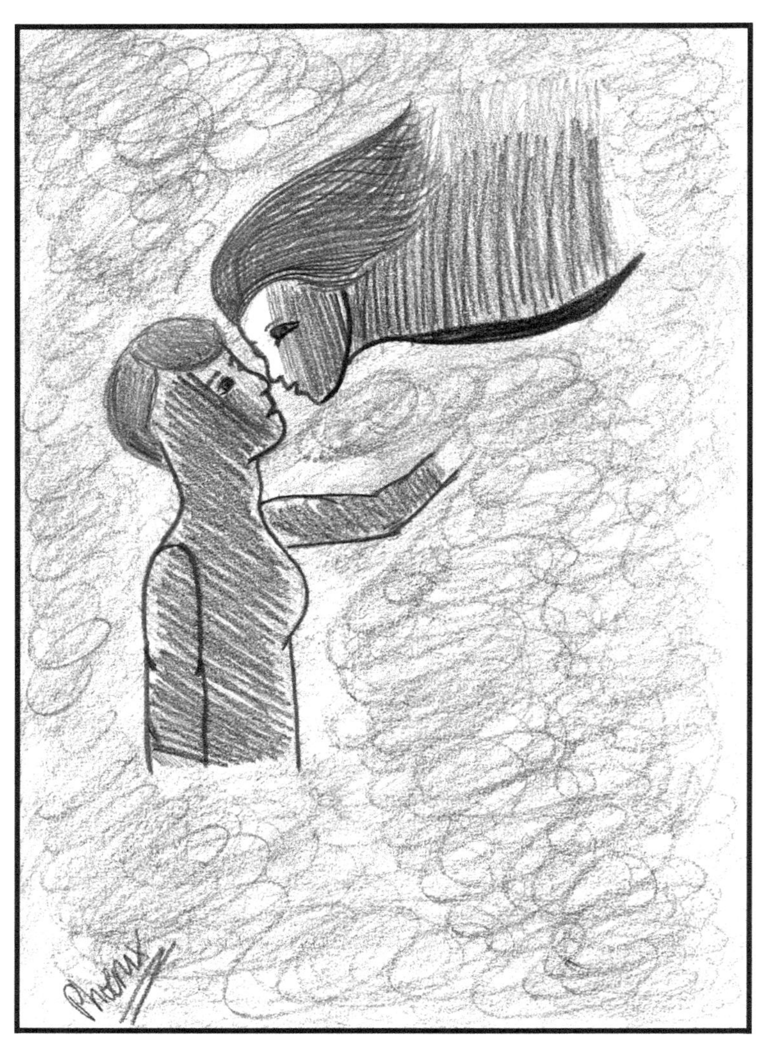

Lovers' Goodbye Kiss

RIVER OF BLACK TEARS

And so he cried a river of black tears
And watched them as they flowed
Wishing he was someplace else
Praying that she'd know

He dug a hole beside her grave
And sang a song of regrets
Then lay his body down beside hers
And wept till nothing was left

All night he stayed by her side
With only the trees lending an ear
To the secrets he whispered to her
Of love, dreams, memories
Of loneliness and fear

Till the setting of the sun
And the rising of it again
He desperately tried to forget the pain
That struck him down, like heavy rain

Yet still it continued to haunt him
Stripping him to his core, to the bone
Leaving him with virtually nothing
Lost, naked, deserted, and alone

All that was left
Was memories of their past
Of autumn evenings and spring vacations
Memories of their sacred love
A love that would always last

So pity him if you will
For the shadows that followed him without mercy
Yet know in your hearts
These shadows that refused to relinquish
Were the relics of his true love – his lady

And though he cried a river of black tears
He smiled as they gently flowed
For in his heart he felt
That she truly did know
Of his love, of their love – of a love that would not die.

There was my world - the hospital time zone I was floundering in—one in which the same routine was repeated day in and day out. Breakfast. Meds. Obs. Lunch. Meds. Obs. Dinner. Meds. Obs. It was an endless time loop in the hospital, with the pristine white walls and the smell of disinfectant. Yet, there was the real world, waiting just outside my window. Only hands grasp away, and unbelievably this world continued while I was left completely shattered, standing in debris and ruins. I was aghast. How could this be? I just needed everything to stop, to pause even for a minute. Give me time to assess the damage, process the trauma, come to terms with my loss. But that's not how the real world works. It never stops. We are all casualties on this never-ending carousel which

Just. Won't. Stop.

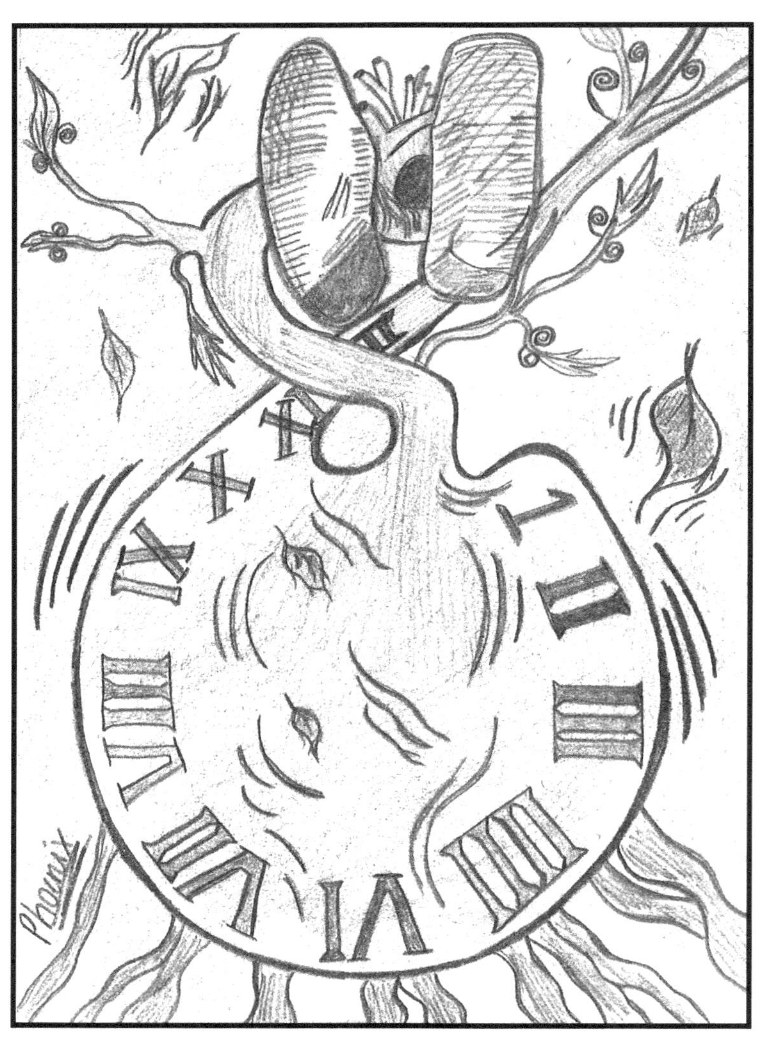

Perpetual Movement

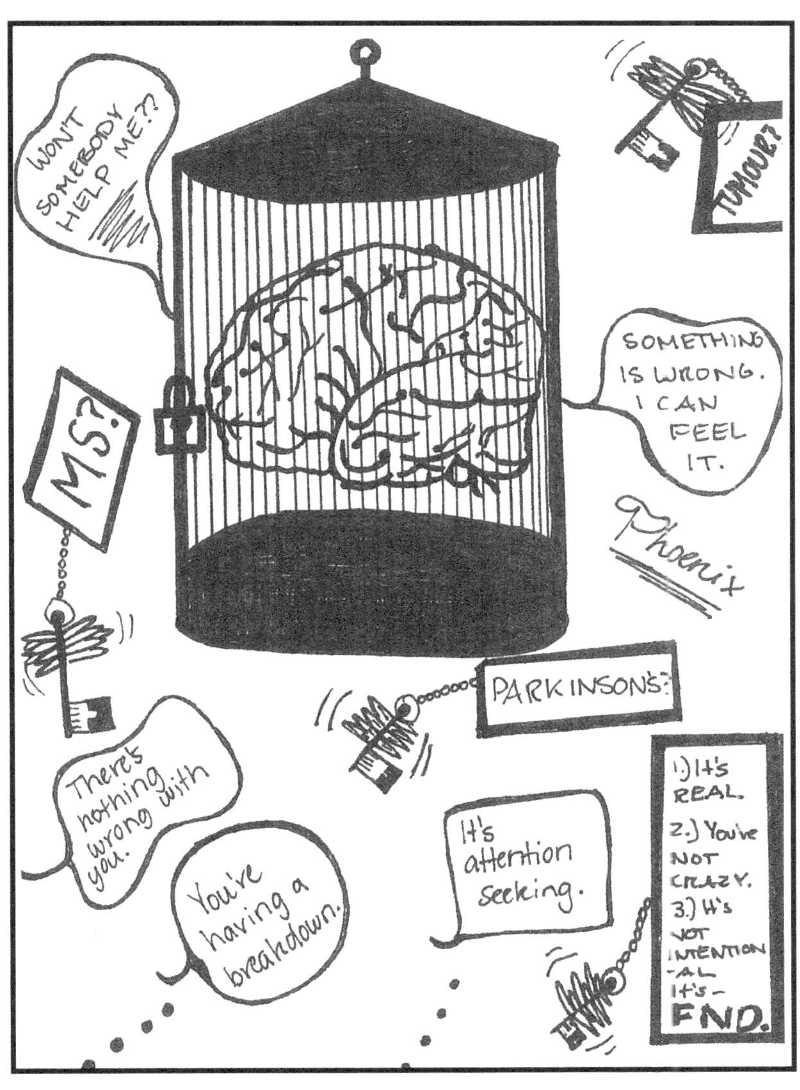

It is a Big Fucking Deal

IT IS A BIG FUCKING DEAL

I can't lift my left leg if I'm lying down.
I can't find my nose or even clap my hands
When my eyes are closed.
I have a constant twitch on the left side of my face,
As well as an intermittent twitch on my right.

But there's nothing wrong with me, Ma.
There's nothing wrong with me.
Or so they keep telling me.

My speech is slurred and I sometimes shutter.
I also have no control of my neck or face movements anymore.
I am a puppet, but where is my master?
Who's pulling my strings?

It's all okay, though, Dad,
Because there's nothing to dismay.
No, there's nothing to dismay.
It's all in working order, or so they say.

My muscles won't listen when I tell them what to do.
"Left leg, move! Brake!" I scream.
Nothing happens. No response.
So now I can't drive.

That's okay, Kellie. No big deal, hey sis?
It's not a big deal. It's not a big deal.
It's all going to be okay.
But that's not how I feel

I have difficulty swallowing now.
Sometimes I can't tell where my limbs start and end.
If I fall asleep, when I wake up, I'm temporarily paralysed
From the neck down.

But oh! How clever I am when I turn on a light!
"Look Dan! I pull this cord and the light goes on!
Isn't that funny? Aren't I clever?"
(Delirium is setting in, can you tell?)

But there ain't a damn thing wrong with me, Dan.
Don't sweat it, brother; nothing to worry about here.
Ain't a damn thing wrong.
At least that's what the doctors have said all along.

I no longer remember the days of the week or the order of events.
Is my birthday the 22nd or 26th of February?
They tell me I'm 29 years old, so really I should know.
I'm trying my hardest, but everything is shifting.

My brain, I can feel it; it's going.
The pressure is building on the left side (I'm in agony!)
Yet the right side is falling asleep or dying.
Why isn't anyone listening to me?

But don't worry, they assured me.
It's just migraines and stress, they said.
Lots of people get twitches.
It's not a big deal. It's not a big deal.

The thing is though,
It WAS a big fucking deal.
It IS a big fucking deal.
It is: Functional Neurological Disorder.

She's got the world on her shoulders; carrying it for the ones she loves.

The load is heavy, and she is weary.

But the wind whispers sweet secrets of hope and peace yet to come.

Thus, she heaves her load and takes another long sigh before looking down the road to walk on by.

The sun is setting on the skyline, its warm glow encompasses her, anc she smiles, as her shadow silently yet persistently follows in her footsteps. Reminding her that she is still her. Despite it all, she is still here.

There's a place I often go

On my own where nobody knows

I close my eyes and count to ten

Before I know it, I'm back there, again.

It's sunny and warm as I stand in the sunshine

It's golden rays shining down on me – the feeling is sublime.

I wrinkle the tips of my toes between the hot grains of sand

Whilst listening to the sea lapping against the shoreland.

I slowly wade in, up to my ankles then knees.

Breathing in deeply, the salty sea breezes.

The sea gulls above soar wild and free

Their calls echo and resonate within me.

Now I am waist high in the ocean's glory

My breaths continue slow and deep as I reflect upon my story.

You see, I come to the sea, to wash away the past.

The mistakes I made, the pain I bare and love that does not last.

These painful stories can never be erased forever for me.

Instead, they are laid to rest in mother nature's waves and taken out to sea.

So, I take a few steps further, towards my fate.

The icy, cold water is lapping across my shoulders now. I don't have much longer to wait.

One more breath in, I fill my lungs with deep, salty air.

Before taking a dive into the next thrashing wave hits me.

Stripping me bare.

It engulfs me. Swallows me whole.

I stay under water as long for as I can. Rekindling the fire in my soul.

I burst through the ocean's surface and gasp for air as the

waves crash against my body.

Each one embracing me. Each one making me stronger.

My heart is racing. It's beating wild and free.

Now I have been washed clean by the deep blue sea.

Then I open my eyes and look around.

I see I am back home, safe and sound.

You see this journey I take is only a shut eye away.

To help with the stress and pain we live with, day to day

Let me be a harbour for you to draw your strength from.

Let me weigh down the anchor in this storm and stand still for you.

My love a beacon in the night.

Sirens calling for sailor's mourning.

My love is unconditional; like a Mother's (love) for her child, so too does mine last a lifetime.

Nor does it have any strings attached. Simply, my beating heart, a reminder:

I am here.

I am here.

PART III

Resurfacing

> But suddenly, a light appeared, shining through.
> The more I wrote and drew,
> this light, it grew and grew,
> and soon I started to rise.
> Resurfacing at last,
> after such a dark demise.

– Exert

As present as she tried to be
One glance and I could see
That she was miles away from me
As her mind drifted across the galaxy.

I saw the planets and shooting stars
Dancing in her eye for hours
Whilst the meteors fell against her hair
Softly and sweetly, like April showers.

Yes, she was far away from here
From all of us on Earth, land and sea.
Living free, detached, and blissfully happy,
Utterly in a world of her own.

And so, I couldn't bear to pull her back
To reality, to society, not even to me.
Not when I saw the peace the galaxy brought her.
Finally, she was home.

The problem with memories is we don't get to choose what our mind remembers. Experiences are imprinted on our brains for different reasons. Try as we might, some scenes will replay again and again, no matter how many times we try to erase them. Whilst others, the ones we treasure: like how it felt when she kissed you, or how your hands fit together perfectly, and you danced every chance you had. Or how she looked most beautiful first thing in the morning, with her messy bed hair, her crooked glasses sitting atop her nose, and those wonderous laugh lines surrounding her eyes. She took your breath away. That, you will never forget. Yet these incredible moments, they sometimes start to fade. Try as we might to hold them, honouring their memory, treasuring their keepsake—our cruel minds have other plans.

Trauma has a stronger imprint, you see. Its mark is toxic and contaminates our head-space. That's why we need to externalise it, talk out loud about the events that haunt us. Otherwise, if we shut down and stay silent, the trauma only exacerbates the fear, darkness, and haunting hold our experience has on us, slowly drawing the life out of us until there's nothing left but an empty, hollow cage of the person we used to be.

Of course, trauma is terrifying. It is debilitating, confronting, challenging, and scary. But it's a part of who we are and the journey we have travelled. We cannot suppress it, deny its existence, or ignore its impact, else we do a grave disservice to ourselves. We reject a part of ourselves, and in doing that we never really move on. Our trauma wins. It consumes us.
So, speak up. Share your story. Externalise your pain suffering. Embrace the darkness inside of you, then let it go and remember:

You survived. You slayed your dragons and defeated the beasts that threatened to destroy you.

Instead, it was you who conquered them.

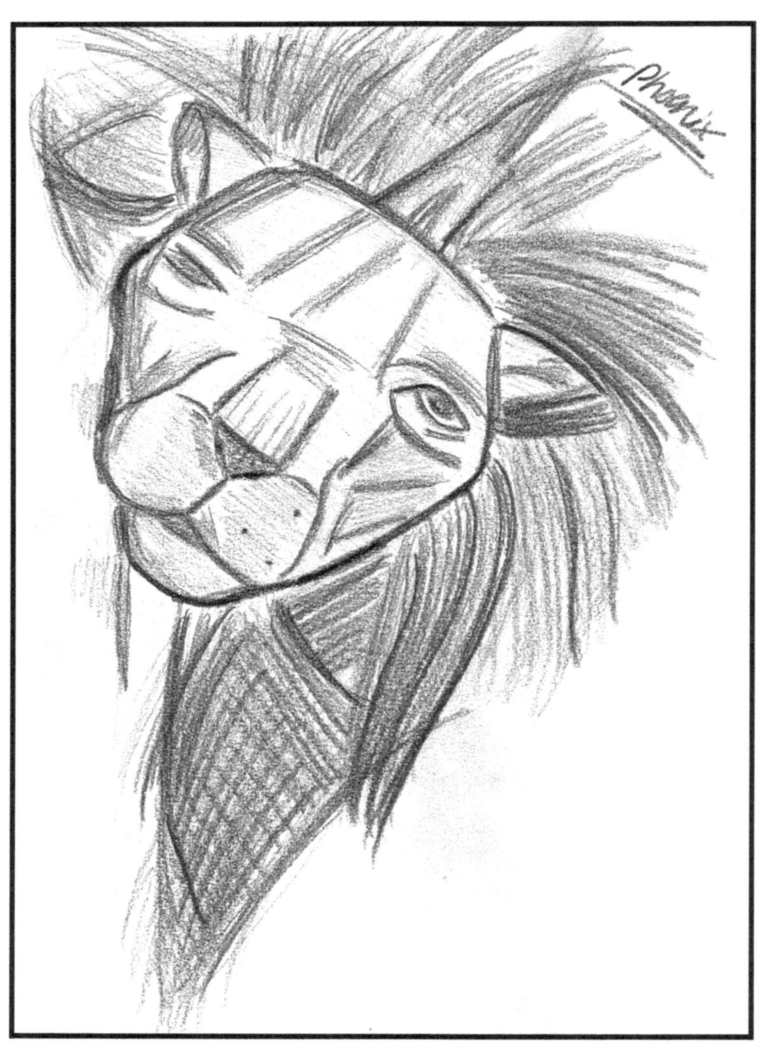

Sleepy Lion

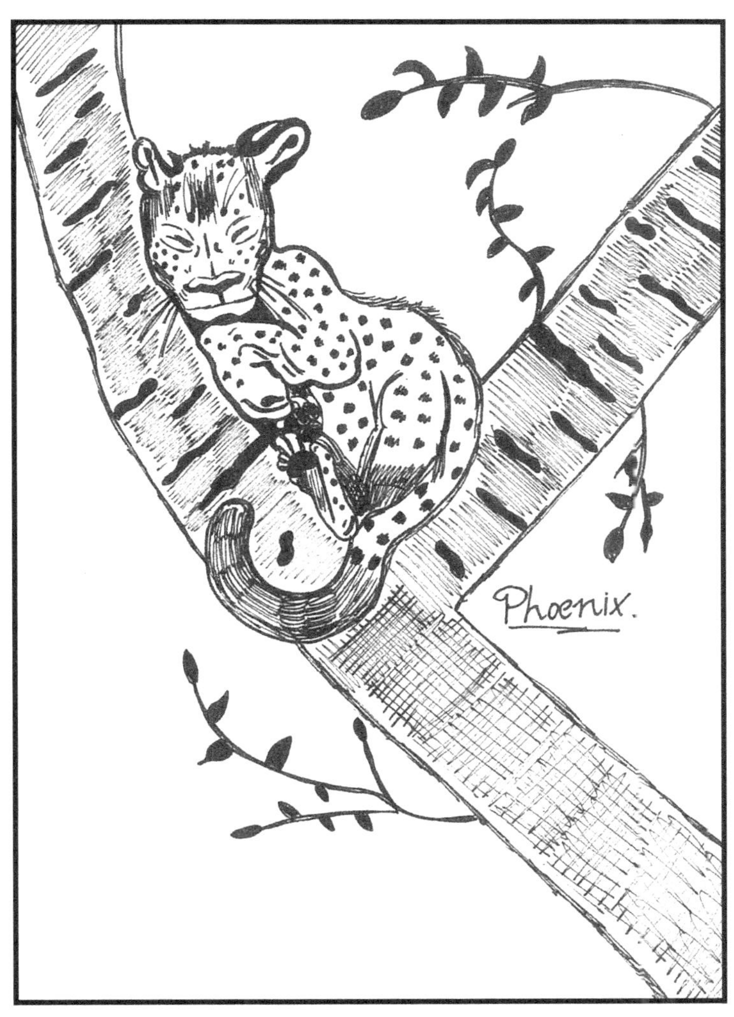

Chee-TAH!

I still write you love letters. I call out your name in the darkness and reach across the sheets, searching for you. I can see your face so clearly on your side of the bed because, after all, it has and always will be yours. Tears roll down my face as yours comes into my line of vision, and I imagine gently holding your face in my hands. I hold you there, frozen in time. It's as though no time has passed at all.

I watch our movies and shows over and over again, laughing and crying in all the same places. It makes me wonder if you feel the same, if you're watching our shows dance across the screen to the rhythm of our memories somewhere else in this madness and chaos.

I wish I'd done more and said more of my thoughts out loud to you. Like how I think you're remarkable, and I love the way you think. How watching the windmills of your mind was exhilarating, and how you always looked your best when you first woke up—messy bed hair, pyjamas, and glasses. I miss making pots of tea for you first thing, and curling up beside you on the couch while you read your book.

That's what love is. The little things that you hardly paid attention to at the time, but now seem so tangible and crucial, you can scarcely breathe when they come to mind.

I miss you just as much as the day you left. I know now more than I did that day. I wish you could see how much I've grown and how much better we would be together now. I'm so sorry for the hurt I caused and the words I left unsaid. For not celebrating every moment like it was our last. For not giving you the room to breathe when you needed it. For not recognising the times for space, and the times to draw you nearer.

I love you just as much now as I did back then, and I doubt that will ever change. You are and always will be my one great love. You complete me. I wish you all the happiness, security, and contentment in the world. I hope we meet again.

Until then, all my love, Madame Phoenix.

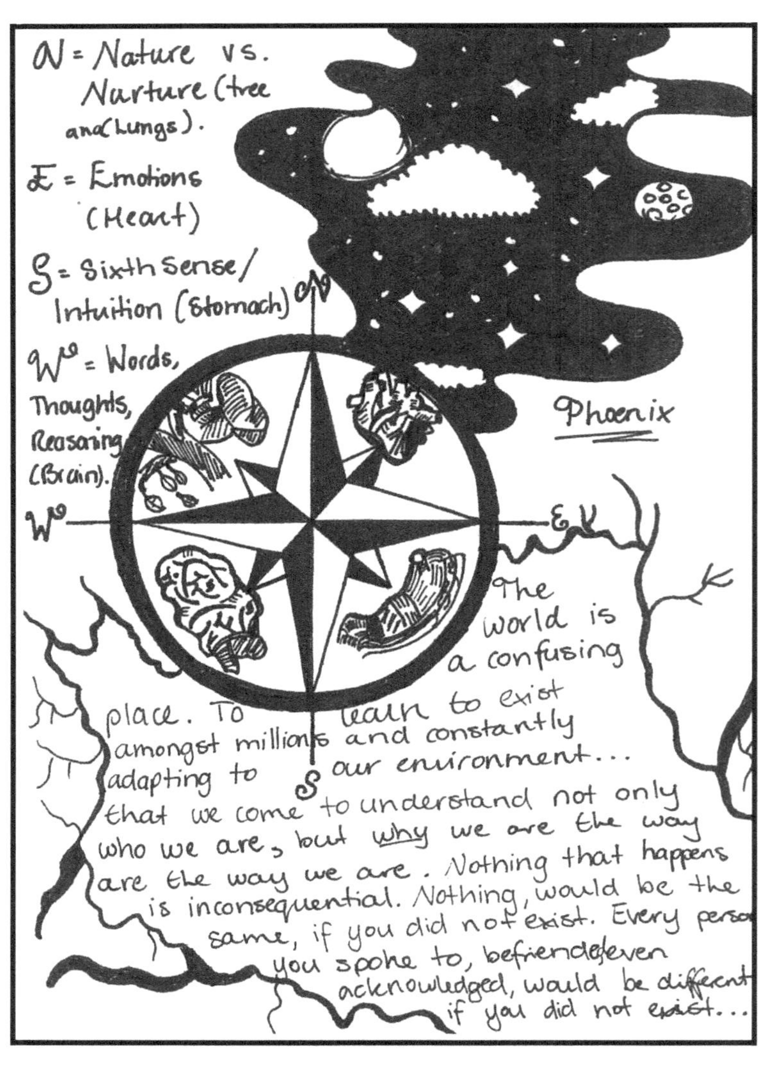

Moral Compass

GRIEF

It's late at night, and the pictures of my past are washing over me like a kaleidoscope of colours. I am filled with grief and wading through memories of the ones I loved who have gone before me.

But that is life and we cannot change it, only adapt and survive. So I shall lay here and watch as these photographs of my mind dance across the starry sky, and feel the music of our exchanges. Embrace the knowledge that these fragments of the people I love who are no longer with me will not wither or waste away. Rather, they shall bear down in my soul, the roots of their being growing deeper and deeper every time I say their names, sing their praises, and tell their stories. That way they will always be here, always with me. That way they will live on, with us all.

I am sorry for the times you did not feel loved or worthy.

That the world had shown you less than you deserved.

I did my best to love you.

To show you every time we touched.

Every time I held you in my arms,

Entwining my body tightly around yours.

Cocooning you from the hurt that came from every direction.

My head was full of whispers,

Thoughts of how I loved, respected, and valued you.

How you were most worthy and wonderful,

Smart and beautiful and funny.

Remarkable, oh, so, remarkable.

So, I'm sorry for the way the world turned its back against you.

And for the times you did not receive the love you deserved.

But I hope you know, each time I held you in my arms,

I was doing my best to show you that I loved you and always would.

I have a jar where I put notes and stories about you and our time together and when I'm sad and lost I sit curled up on the couch and read them to myself. To remind me of how remarkable we were and the many adventures we had together. We were soaring to new heights across the skies, deep below the valleys and way across the meadows. Oh yes, we were soaring but now, I fly solo.

The drums inside my head are pounding,
beating like crashing waves.
Ocean resounding
to the calls of sirens, of home I desperately crave.

My heart is heavy,
sinking for the burdens I carry.
They weigh me down like an anchor.
Past traumas chained to my feet drag behind me.

I am sinking,
drowning under the heaviness of it all.
I have sunk to the depths where
no one can find me.

Curled up like a baby, trying to find solace
like I once had in my mother's womb.
But all there is is darkness.
It coils around my body until it is all I am – I am entombed.

It suffocates me. A sinkhole in the ocean.
Except it's one inside my head.
This is my depression.
This is what it's like to live inside my head.

I hear the people calling aboveground.
Their voices are muffled and faint,
like they're talking under water – distorted and sprawling.

I yearn to respond, but I can't move, much less make a sound.
Instead my body tightens, turns further within itself.
The darkness holds me tighter still.

The sirens calling me home grow fainter still.
These walls of depression and madness are my new normal.
I nestle in as best I can and do my utmost to fight against the chill.
Resigning myself to the place I must now call my home.

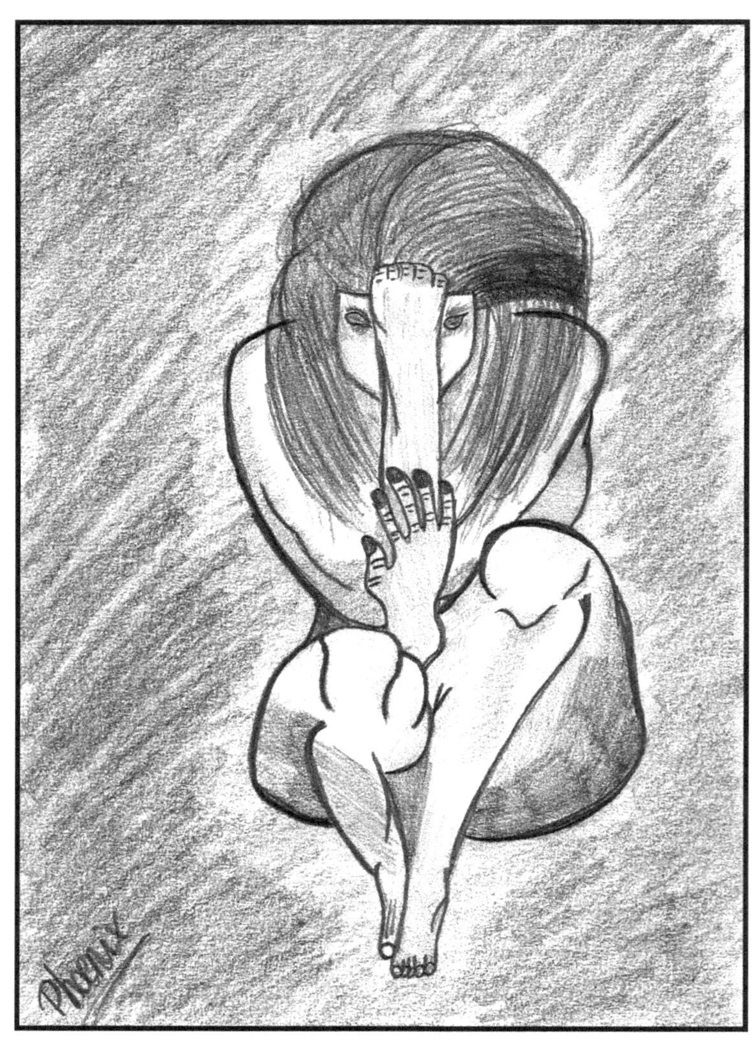

Warrior at Rest

INNER TURMOIL

The inner turmoil you face each day
Is hidden from the rest of the world
You're fighting the storm, all alone
And all you want to do is run away.

Newspaper lands on your doorstep
The coffee brews, but your cup is already full of regrets
The sun begins to set and soon the moon will rise
Flowers will bloom as you say your goodbyes.

Last night's memories bring yesterday's news
Your ex-partner still loves you, but you don't fit the shoes
So you disconnect the phone and draw up an empty chair
As you scream into the deafening silence, praying someone's there.

The voices in your head tell you to end it all
Room is spinning faster; you're trapped within these walls
Everything moves in slow motion; you're losing what you once gained
The storm is taking over; just let go, let go of all this pain.

Back door slams; she's returned once more
It's no surprise to her; you're lying naked on the floor
Self-destruction is your friend; bones from the closet dispersed everywhere
Nevertheless, she picks you up and wipes your bloodshed tears.

The inner turmoil you face each day
Is not as hidden as you would like to believe
You're fighting the storm, but not alone
She's always there; she's all you know.

So take her hand and feel her embrace
Face the darkness and learn to stand
Your smile's a little crooked, but she doesn't care
Coffees boiled; regrets are nowhere to be found.

The sun sets and the stars begin to shine
God has granted you one more dime
Remember you're fighting the storm, but not alone
She's always there; she's all you know.

We are no more than mere puppets in this charade of existence.
Watch as Master forces us to dance with constant persistence.
We are pulled in directions relentlessly with no say.
Our rebellion and resistance ignored every blasted day.
Dance ballerina! Dance, dance; make Master proud.
Pull in his direction, but hide your fury from the crowd.
Stretched far and thin, there is nothing to be done.
These are the roles we must play – the show must go on.
You can scream, cry, weep, and protest.
From the rising of the sun until the time it sets.
Alas, my comrades, it will not make any difference.
For our fates are sealed. We are exploited and helpless.
Dance ballerina! Dance, dance; make Master proud.
Pull in his direction, but hide your fury from the crowd.

HAVE YOU HEARD THE NEWS TODAY?

Have you heard the news today?
Another child has gone away.
They've disappeared, never to be seen again.
Their parents left with nothing but anguish and pain.

Have you heard the news today?
A young woman committed suicide.
Her friends and family are devastated.
Questions unanswered about the darkness inside her she managed to hide.

Have you heard the news today?
Another shooting in a school has taken place.
Blood and bodies discarded without regard.
Is there no mercy? Is there no grace?

Have you heard the news today
About the wars across the seas?
Men, women, and children are dying.
Will our world ever be at peace?

Have you heard the news today?

It just gets worse, day by day.

We bury our heads and convince ourselves

there's nothing we can do.

But the truth is, we can and should.

If we gave a damn at all for our fellow man, for me and for you.

So, will you?

Have you heard the news today?

It's not too late to have your say.

Or would you prefer to look the other way?

Have you heard the news today?

She had always lived her life in a cage.

When she was younger, she was forced to build one out of necessity.

To protect herself from the monsters who had, or were going to do, her harm.

This cage was a fortress made of steel iron and kept the monsters at bay.

But unfortunately, it also kept everyone else at bay.

The ones she loved. The ones she held most dear.

But she had no choice.

At least that's what her fear told her.

However, over recent years, she learnt to build a new cage.

One, which was just as safe but was beautiful and safe and,

She could come and go as freely as she liked.

She could keep out the evil doers but let her loved ones in.

Boundaries. That's what she learnt all the years on.

She built a cage with boundaries.

To keep her safe.

It was still lonely.

She continued to feel the need to keep others at safe distance,

and perhaps, she will never love again,

The way she loved you.

But at least she's safe now and can see all the world's wonders.

From her beautiful cage upon the hill and can come and go at her own free will

People say there are five stages of grief. Denial. Anger. Bargaining. Depression. Acceptance.

As humans we like to simplify. To compartmentalize things into nice small boxes we can pack away and hide so we don't have to look at them. To think about or recognise or acknowledge their presence in our lives or, in the case of grief, the lives they took. But as someone who has experienced immense grief and I'm talking tidal wave, complete ocean of wrath of grief that brought me down to my bare bones. I can assure you. There is no such thing as five stages of grief.

The mere idea is too simplistic. It belittles and disparages the trauma one lives through when they lose the person, thing or sometimes place they love and hold dearly. No. Their grief cannot be measured solely by five stages. Rather there are moments. Fleeting moments that come in aftershocks hitting you repeatedly. Millions of moments of emotions you didn't even know existed, let alone, know that you could feel. Repeatedly and often overlapping so much you can scarcely breathe. You feel shades of moods so variant that Picasso pales in comparison to you.

Denial, anger, bargaining, depression, and acceptance. These are simply umbrellas to encompass our incredulous colours of emotions we feel when we lose something or someone we love. When we have lost something that is inside of us A part of us that makes us who we are that we can know longer have or hold onto. When we feel that pain. That absence of the piece of puzzle that makes up a part of who we are. When we say good-bye to that someone or something - that is when, we feel it. A million moments of grief.

Hurt. Confusion. Lost. Begging. Desperation. Pain. Sorrow. Sadness. Weeping. Loneliness. Doubt. Disbelief. Pleading. Reminiscing. Unconsumable rage. Blame. Despair. Heartache. Desolate. Anguish. Emotional. Irritational. Erratic. Blind with anger. Wretched. Tortured. Distressed. Lament. Howling constantly - in the shower, in the car, doing the dishes, listening to certain songs and into the night. Broken-hearted. Inconsolable. Bewildered. Drowning. Depressed. Remorseful. Oh, the remorse and regret – it eats you alive from the inside out.

The list goes on and it is, long and unforgiving. Not only that but it's not nice and linear as depicted by the medical field. It's chaos. An ambush. You're drudging through the drenches whilst every emotion lies in wait like a grenade hidden across enemy lines which you're desperately trying to avoid at all costs. But you can't. Because that's not how grief works. That's not what mourning looks or sounds like. It's bawling your eyes out in the bath as the boiling hot water pelts across your back and you're slamming your fists against the shower wall. It's avoiding familiar places because they're too painful to return too. It's screaming into your pillow in the early hours of the morning as your night terrors haunt you of the loss you are mourning, and you can hardly see that shred of light breaking through your bedroom curtains like a whimsical promise you only hear about in folk lore and fairy tales.

But you keep going despite the million moments of grief. You drudge through the trenches, wiping the sludge off your forehead as you try your best to live not day to day. Oh no, that's far too difficult at this point; instead, you live hour by hour or minute by minute. Whatever works for you on this long, rocky road. You sweat, strain, and charge forward as best you can and you learn; you learn, to live, with the abundant of emotions that shadow you for who knows how long. You live, with the million moments of grief, because that's what you must do. It's the only choice there is.

PART IV

Floundering

> Struggling still, I floundered about,
> the obstacles I faced with determination and strong will.

– Exert

I wish you happiness
if only for a while.
I wish you always find
a reason to smile.

I wish you sunshine
to chase away the rain.
As well as family and friends
to take away your pain.

I wish you may learn
to love yourself for who you really are.
Love with all your heart
if only from afar.

I wish you may listen
to the wind that gently blows,
whispering secrets of life and love,
secrets we all crave to know.

I wish that you may always have
your hopes and dreams to hold.
No matter how hard life gets
or what you may be told.

So, I wish you happiness
if only for a while.
And I wish you may always have
a reason to smile.

I wish you sunshine
to chase away the rain.
Plus, family, friends, and even strangers
to take away the pain.

But most of all, I wish that you may learn to love and accept yourself, for all of who
you are.
And love with all your heart, with everything you have
if only from afar.

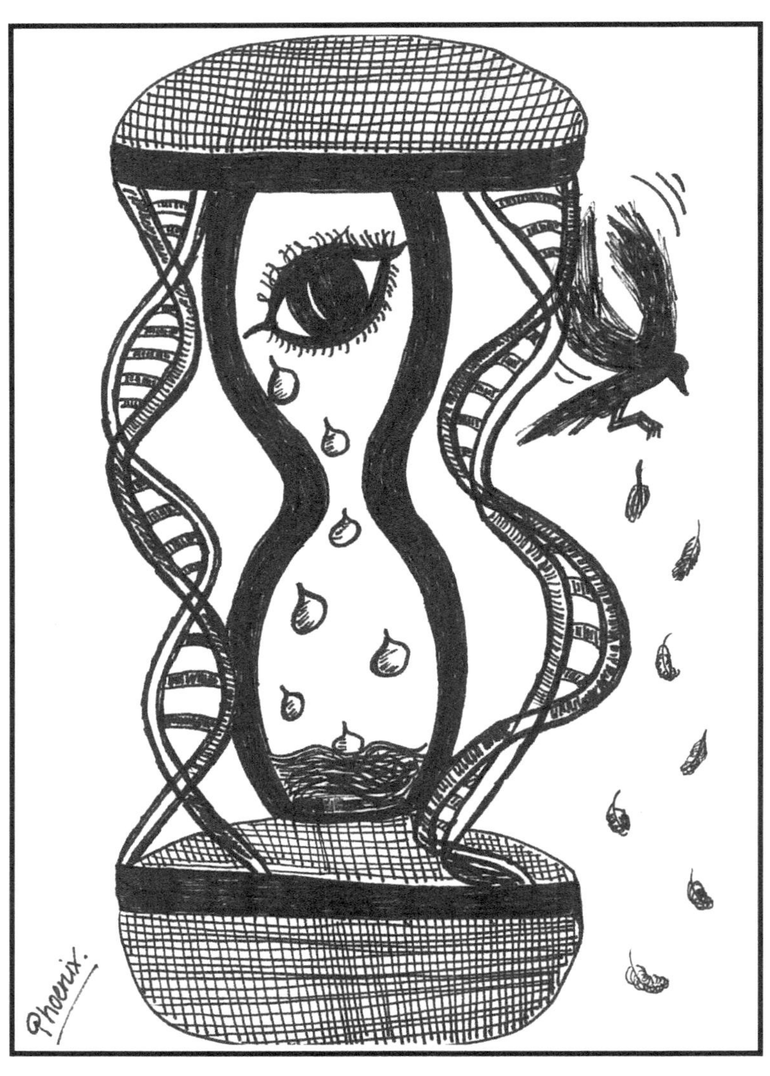

Death Calling

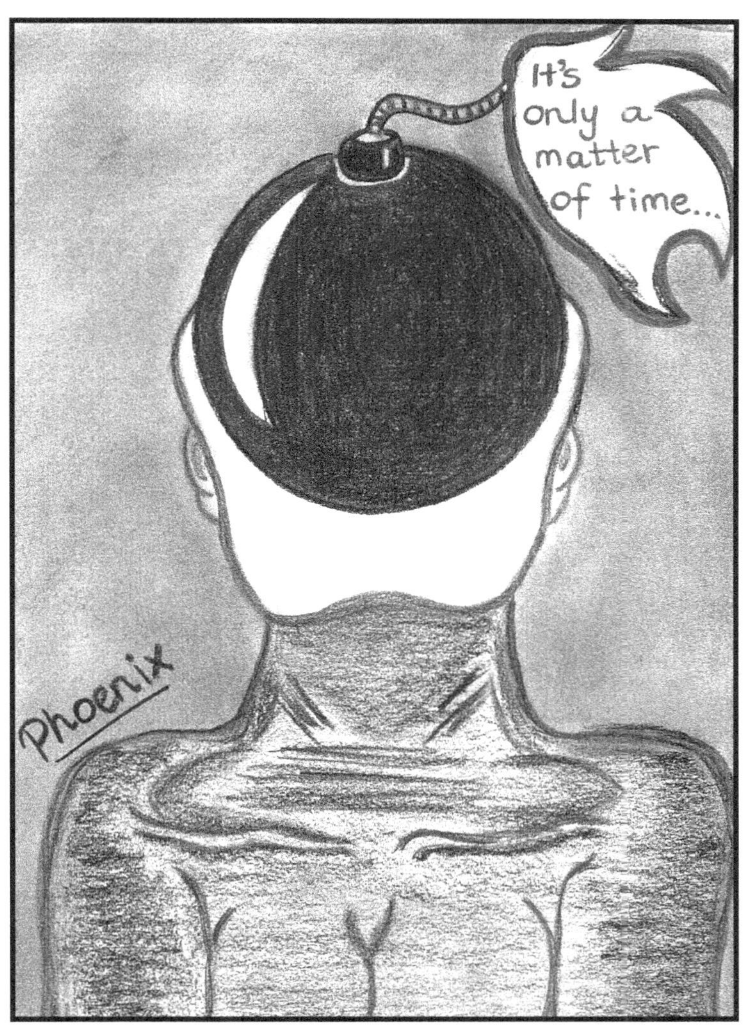

It's only a matter of time

We're all at the point of no return,
Balancing on the precipice of reason and insanity.
It's only a matter of time before the dice is rolled.
Before our final hand is dealt.
Before our head explodes and nothing remains
but ashes and dust,
Mere fragments of the individuals we once were,
Disappeared into thin air, soon to be forgotten.
Though we long to be remembered.
It's only a matter of time.

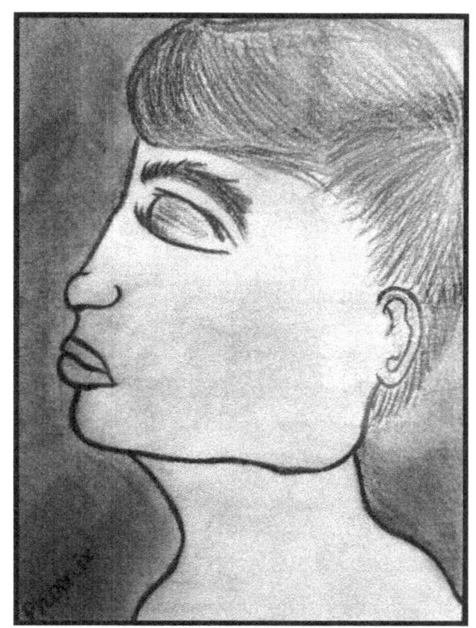

Sweet Release

We are but a bundle of emotions, constantly moving and changing to the rhythm of life. We adapt and steer our ship as best we can to stay on course, but sometimes life will hit us hard with turmoil, storms, and devastation.

The faces you see are never all that is to be seen. They are merely the tip of the iceberg. Like a child's behaviour, we often have to dig deeper to understand what someone is feeling and experiencing.

Don't be afraid to ask. Don't hold back. Reach out and ask the much-needed questions. It starts with "Are you okay?" and hopefully ends with "What can I do?" and "I am here for you".

Be present. Be vigilant. Be considerate. It only takes a moment to check on someone and that single moment can make all the difference in someone's life.

What are you waiting for? What have you got to lose?

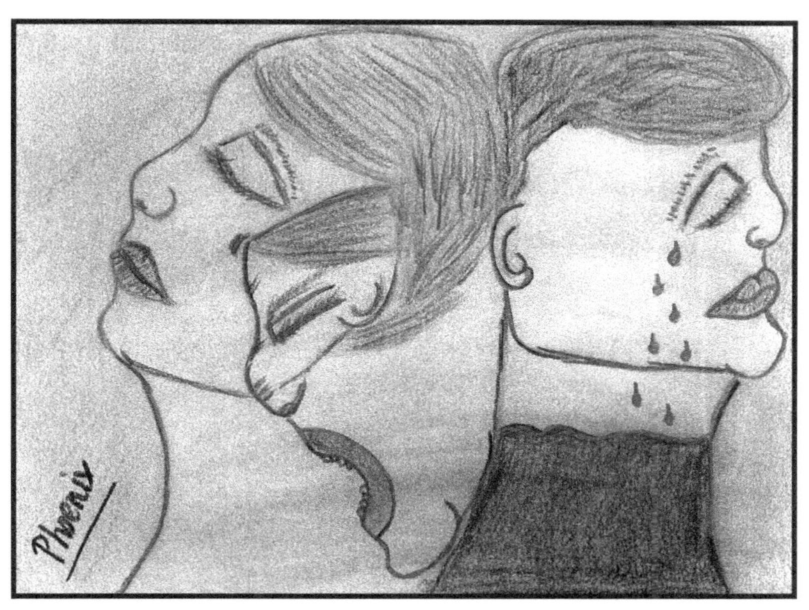

Tormented Soul

WE ARE NOT OKAY.

BREAK THE SILENCE — RAP

CHORUS
We are not okay. We are not okay.
Yeah, our minds are starting to rot,
they're starting to decay
from the abuse and suffering
we subject them to every damn day.
We're a mess. We're a mess.
Walls are caving in; the whole world's in distress.
Mental illness is all around us.
It's time to break the silence.

MALE
I'm a freak. I'm alone.
I am weak. No one's home.
I've been left to fight this war
inside my head, inside my head.
I am walking, yet I'm the living dead.
I've been left to fight this war
But what and for whom am I fighting for?

CHORUS
We are not okay. We are not okay.
Yeah, our minds are starting to rot,
they're starting to decay

from the abuse and suffering

we subject them to every damn day.

We're a mess. We're a mess.

Walls are caving in; the whole world's in distress.

Mental illness is all around us.

It's time to break the silence.

FEMALE

I am helpless.

I've gone mad.

The voices in my head are relentless

and I'm so misunderstood and sad.

There are no more words left to speak.

For the company I had, I no longer keep.

I am abandoned, isolated, adrift.

A loose cannon, a lost star, invisible and misfit.

What am I waiting for?

I can't stand this war. I can't stand this war.

CHORUS

We are not okay. We are not okay.

Yeah, our minds are starting to rot,

they're starting to decay.

from the abuse and suffering

we subject them to every damn day.

We're a mess. We're a mess.

Walls are caving in; the whole world's in distress.

Mental illness is all around us.

It's time to break the silence.

So let me hear you scream and yell.

Tear these walls down to hell.

Break the stigma, set us free

as we watch our demons flee.

Break the silence. Break the silence.

Fight with us. Yeah, join our alliance

in this war against mental illness and the stigma it draws.

Join the fight, fight the war.

Come on now,

what are you waiting for?

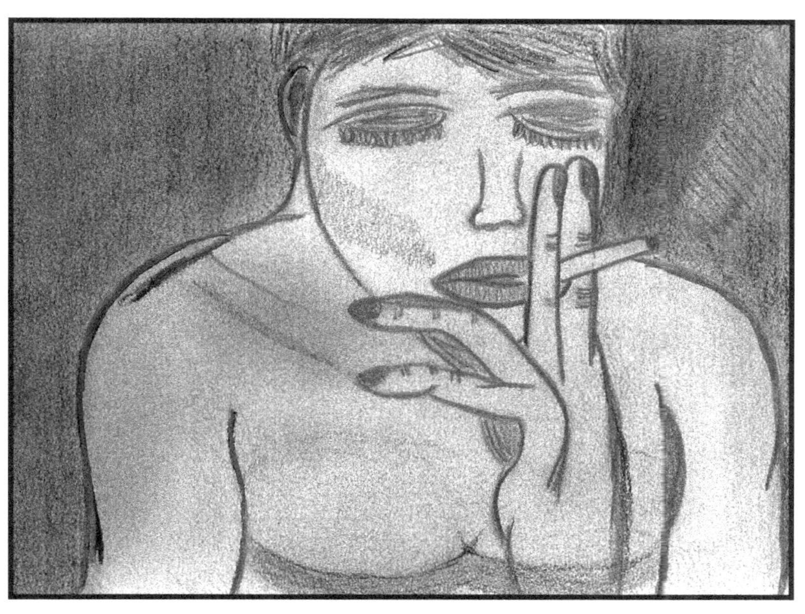

She chose the green over red any day of the week

PART V

Treading Water

Soon I found my rhythm, the words I wrote were music etched deep
within my soul that I could dance to.
The artwork I sketched was my heartbreak and trauma I could work
through.

- Exert

I thought I gave my all, but time, wisdom, and maturity have taught me that I could have done more. I could have been more open. More assertive. More respectful of your boundaries and need for space.
I could have done more but know, at the time, I gave you everything I knew I had.
I loved you to the best of my ability.

I loved you with all my heart, and still, to this day, have that love running deep for you. Always.

The world is a confusing place. To learn to exist amongst millions of others and constantly evolving and adapting to our environment. Every person, each experience we encounter impacts us. We are sponges – forever soaking up everything around us and, try as we might, we can never completely erase or wash what once was. We aren't even always aware of how events change us. It's only when time goes by or a stressful event occurs, causing a trigger reaction that was learnt long agon, that we come to understand not only who we are, but why we are the way we are. Nothing that happens is inconsequential. Nothing would be the same if you did not exist. Every person you met, whether it's strangers, friends, colleagues, loved ones; each person you spoke to, befriended, even acknowledged, would be different if you did not exist. We are not here on Earth as mere empty vessels to fill a space or play an offside character in someone else's story. Individually we are intricately woven. The blueprints of our minds, our hearts, bodies, and souls are complex beyond comprehension. You, as an individual are extraordinary and fascinating and powerful! You are invaluable and worthy and there is no one else like you.

You are more than what happened to You. You are more than the past you have survived; the stories you have lived and the words that have been spoken for and against you. You are more thank your mistakes and your successes. Your choices and actions speak volumes and create ripples in hundreds of people's lives every day. The world would not be the same without you. The people in your life would not be the same. Their lives, their stories would change; irrevocably. You are more than you can possibly fathom. But most of all:

You are more than enough.

Hey there, Benny Boy,
what's on your mind tonight?
Your eyes are darker than the nightfall's sky.
Oh, what's the story, Benny?
What's given you a fright?
Come closer, Benny Boy, my child.
Oh, it's going to be all right.
I promise everything's goin' to be all right.

Did your mamma hurt you, boy
when she hit your daddy so?
Did her raging temper scare you
as she let all self-control go?
Or was it the words that cut you to the core?
Oh tell me, Benny, can you take much more?
Yeah, tell me child, can you take much more?

Oh Benny, you know she didn't mean it, see,
when she said you weren't meant to be?
Yeah, Benny, you know that was the vodka's part
that poisoned her tongue and broke your heart.
Oh Benny, don't get wasted, don't let your body go.
The streets are not for you, boy, they can't help you, no.
Come on, Benny Boy, take my hand and let's go home.
I know tonight will get worse, but it's better than being alone.
And don't forget, Benny Boy, your baby sister needs you home.

Hey Benny, does it make you feel angry and wild

the way your mamma treats you and pushes you aside?

Or are you too busy trying to play father

to your sister who hides beneath the covers?

Talk to me, boy; tell me what it's like

to live in a house where nothing is right.

Where the sun doesn't shine, and the darkness always stays.

Tell me, Benny Boy, do you think God hears your prayers?

Dry your tears, Benny boy, please let me hold you so.

That flask in your hand won't drown your sorrows.

It'll only bring you pain of yesterday and tomorrow.

Oh, Benny, baby, don't get wasted, don't let your body go.

The streets are not for you boy, they can't help you, no.

Come on, Benny Boy, take my hand, let's go home.

Lean on me, come now, here's my sleeve.

Wipe your tears, please don't grieve.

I know your mamma hurts you and your daddy doesn't care,

but Benny, please stay strong, cause your sister needs you there.

Oh Benny, I know it isn't fair, and I know this isn't right.

Come closer, Benny, I'm going to sit with you till morning light.

Yeah Benny Boy, everything's going to be okay.

I'm not going anywhere. I'm staying right here with you.

Going to be here till night is through.

Have you ever stayed awake at night
listening to the sound of falling rain?
Wishing and praying with all your might
that it would wash away your pain?

Have you turned your face to the night sky
to stare at the full moon aglow?
Asking God, "What will become of me?"
His reply: "Child, if only you could know…"

Have you ever wept and cried to yourself from sunset to sunrise?
Bargaining with the ones above
to no avail or surprise.

Or have you ever replayed memories
over and over and over again?
Images so fleeting, it atrophies.
You lose yourself; you're going round the bend.

If you have then you know just as well as I
there is no end to this madness or existence.
The carousel keeps turning until the day we die.
We are prisoners of this world, despite our resistance.

So, close your eyes and get some sleep
whilst you listen to the falling rain.
Dream of better days and do not weep
as tomorrow brings hope and a chance to start again.

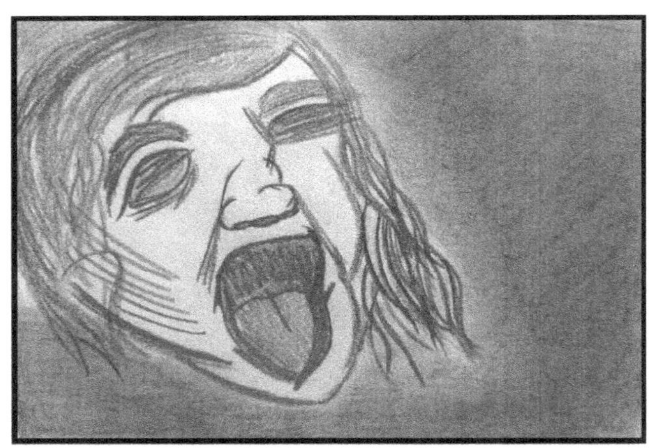

Let Me Go

Thoughts are reeling, my mind, unweaving
from memories of what used to be.
Despondent and haunting; my heart is concealing
this burning passion within.

Leave me be.
Let me die.
Leave to ruin
What must lie.

Dark and twisted, the snowflakes they kiss me,
Washing away the tears of blood I cry.
I fall and stumble; my body it crumbles
as I sink in the unforgiveable snow.
The blizzard, it breaks me. Nothing can save me.
It's over. I'm gone. Let me go.

To the tired and weary,

I'm going to keep this short because you need the no-beating-around-the-bush approach. It's okay that you are NOT okay.

It's okay that you're scared, sad, and lonely, but also relieved, grateful, and at times abundantly happy. These are a lot of emotions to be feeling, and to be feeling them all at once is intense and overwhelming. You've been through trauma and hardships—some old, some new.

But there is hope. There is recovery and light and healing. There is no end date. I cannot ease your suffering by telling you when this dark time will pass and you will be able to breathe again. We have to be patient and take one step at a time. Just as long as you remember: it's okay to not be okay, but one day you will be. One day, you will find peace and joy and contentment. You will dance, sing, and smile because you deserve it. You are more than enough, and you will not be defined by the pain you suffer or the trauma you experience. So be patient, young one, and please be kind, gentle, and loving to yourself. You deserve it. You are more than enough. Trust me. Have faith.

From someone who has and continues to survive the path of darkness and is stronger, wiser, and better for it.

Madame Phoenix

I stand before you resolute.

Years of experience worn on my shoulders like badges of honour.

Don't underestimate me. I will defy the odds and break free from whatever cage society or my own body endeavours to encompass me in.

I've learnt to break the locks and changed that once entangled me.

I cannot be imprisoned.

I am a bird meant to fly free above the horizon and the mountain tops.

Across the wide, open seas and valleys that resonate the liberty that burns within me.

Do not underestimate me. For I will soar higher than the hawks and farther than the eye can see.

This is me. This is me.

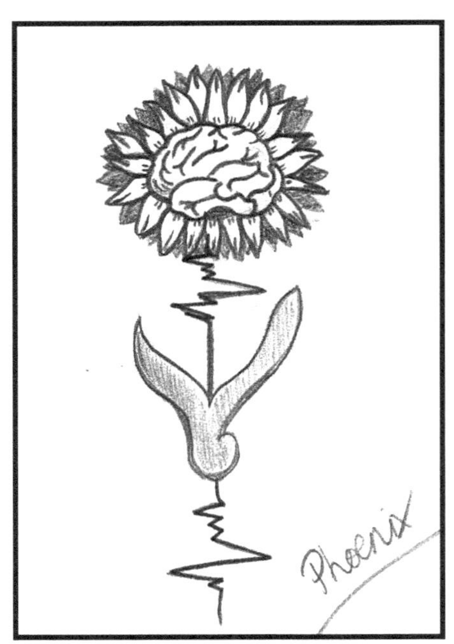

Mental Illness and FND Tattoo Design

You taught me how to wonder

About the way things worked and how things came to be

You taught me how to play, to dance, to sing.

To think outside the box, to question what I thought, saw, felt. Everyth ng.

You opened my eyes to a world I'd run away from for oh so long.

I had let that taste of adventure lie dormant for so many years.

You invited me into the magic of existence again and made me feel like I belonged.

I unleashed my inhibitions, closed my eyes, savored my freedom, and said goodbye to my fears.

Together we reached for the sky, chasing the clouds, while the others gazed from below.

We were in our element, our own world, living in the now with no regrets.

They shook their heads with disappointment, knowing there was nothing they could do.

We were lost together. We were happy and content. We treasured every moment.

Now time has passed us by. We're on different sides of the world, universes apart.

Though sometimes at night I can still reach for you in the dark and feel the beating of your heart.

You're lying next to me, like you did for so many nights long, long ago.

Yes, you may be miles away from me, but in my mind and body, I never really let you go.

I miss listening to your stories, hearing your adventures when you were younger, and seeing all the photos of your antique collections. The beautiful vases and bottles were exquisite. We had that in common: our love of history and old relics from the past. We both loved Edith Piaf, and I'll never forget how chuffed you were when I gave you my old CDs of hers because I was a "trendy young lass" who listed to music on "that new modern thing" (Spotify). I think of you every time I hear her sing.

I loved watching your face light up every time you talked about your family; you were so proud of them all. Always the family man. Showing me photos of your kids and grandkids and the driveway you helped pave for your daughter. "I still got it in me," you said so proudly. And so you did. You were so full of life.

You were a great friend to me, perhaps more than you ever realised. Always there when I needed someone to talk to. Telling me, "You'll see. It's going to be okay. Give it time." That I was strong, and I had more strength, determination, and fire than I knew, but I just had to "lean into it and trust myself. Be the Madame Phoenix. Rise again." Your words surround me like beating drums, echoing the sound of my heart as it pushes against the tide of life we're all swimming up against. The ocean of grief that swallowed me in those years after the accident.

You saw how it broke me. Wearing me down each day. Every challenge like a wave crashing and thumping against my body as it stumbled and tumbled again and again. Struggling to keep my head above it all, to keep from drowning. So many times, I wanted to give up. To just let go and let myself sink to the bottom of the darkness. Let its coldness encase me completely for the last time.

But people like you in my life were like rays of light reaching down, calling to me. Embers and flickers of flame burning at the soles of my feet, keeping me warm and slowly heating up the fire within me that you knew I had. The fire that would rise again and burn all the anger, hurt, grief, heartache, and chaos to the ground so I could rise from the ashes and start anew. Your words and friendship sustained me in a time of my life where everything was falling apart and I was faced with constant loss and destruction. But you were there. You made me laugh. You told me stories. We shared our love of Edith Piaf and traded books at the pub. I will treasure these memories for as long as I live.

I know you're still looking out for me, and I bet you're looking down on us all whilst enjoying a beer from your barstool up in the skies. I only hope you'll save a seat next to you, because one day I'll be joining you, and I look forward to sitting with you once again, old friend.

Love, Madame Phoenix

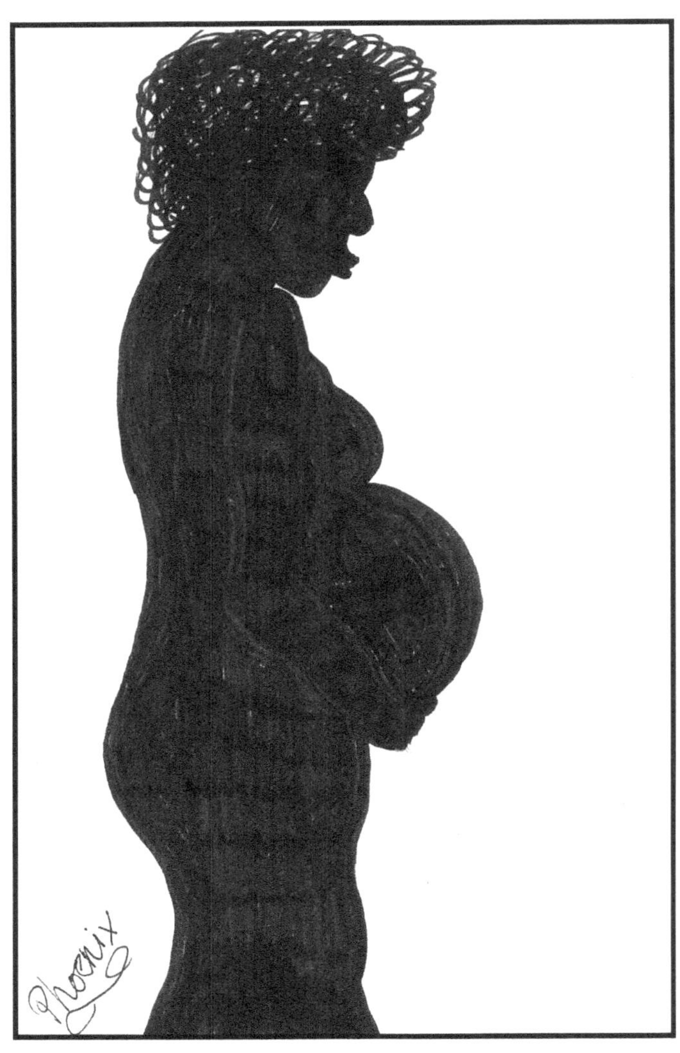

Precious

Hush now, be still, oh tired and weary one.

Let go, leave all thoughts to yesterday

and dream as night has come.

The journey you're on is long but you are not alone.

We have many paths to tread.

Many things yet to be said and done.

Rest, love, I'll draw you near and hold your hand

as we travel together across these known lands.

Where the road will lead us remains uncertain and unclear,

but I promise you as long as we're together, there is nothing to fear.

Shush now, it's time to sleep, close your eyes and drift away.

Let go, my love, of all your worries. They have no cause to stay.

May the magic nightlife shelter us once again.

Until the dawn breaks and greets us

with home, like an old friend.

PART VI

Swimming, Gazing

I lay on my back, smiling as the sun kissed my cheeks, and the ocean
lapped at my thighs.
I turned my head from the shoreline back to the sunshine and blue
skies.
Tears rolled down my face as I gently whispered to myself,
"You did it. You survived."

– Exert

I have many stories to tell. I have had grand adventures, slayed dragons and defeated giants, and I have lived to tell the tale. I've had heartbreak and grief as well as immense joy and fulfilment.

I have met so many people. Some have been kind and left me with love. Others have been cruel and left me with lessons.

That's okay because it's part of my history, my story, my love, my life, and my soul. I can't escape it and I no longer need to. I am proud and loving of who I am. I accept all that I am, and I know that I have become this person today because of the paths I've crossed, the people I've met, and the experiences I've had.

But I also have regrets. There are many things in my life that I would do differently. And I think it's okay to know, accept, and want both.

I am okay with that now.

You are more than the past you have survived, the stories you have lived, and the words that have been spoken to, for, and against you. You are more than your mistakes and your successes. Your choices and actions speak volumes and create ripples in hundreds of people's lives every day.

The world would not be the same without you. The people in your life would not be the same. Their lives and their stories would change irrevocably. You are more than you can possibly fathom.

You think death scares me?
There are worse things in life to be feared.
Things like knowing you've lost your best friend
or the love of your life.
Of living your life without reaching your potential.
Hiding in the shadows.
Too afraid to own who you are for fear of rejection.

FATHER'S DAY POEM

When we were young children
You taught us the magic of possibilities
To achieve greatness
To constantly strive for endlessly opportunities.

You were our captain
The commander of our ship
Cheering us on and steering our voyage
Through the good, the bad, and the hardships.

At swimming carnivals, you fiercely charged
Beside the pool as we swam and competed
Proudly calling out to us,
"Look forward! Don't be defeated!"

Before and after school sports, choir, band practice and music lessons
Were all accompanied and chauffeured by you
In the dingy Magna with its sunken roof
With your knee-high socks and propeller hat
And a newspaper in tow
Your trademarks through and through.

You were a man of few words back then and brew and stew you often would
However, beneath this grizzly bear appearance
Your devotion and love were never questioned
It was always there and understood.

You taught us how to persist and to be resilient
To cast our nets wide, harness our anchor, and maintain our course
To face life's challenges and navigate through the storm
You taught us to be our own hero, forever strong, a driving force.

Now our days together are still cherished as father and daughter, father and son
We are so blessed to also have the honour and privilege of calling you our friend
Someone who can walk alongside us until the going down of the sun.

THE LITTLE RED STRING —

A SHORT STORY

My heart is as vast as the bright blue sky, and my love runs deeper than the valleys and is stronger than the currents down the rivers. I place my hands on my chest and feel my heart beating, and as I do, I see something small, wavering in the wind. It is bright and delicate, yet strong like rope. I squint and see that it is a long piece of red braided string, made from the strongest, finest, and softest twine.

I pull on it gently, and I feel an ache in my chest, as though someone's reached in and squeezed my heart tightly with both hands. I look down closer and follow the piece of string back to its starting point, only to find it's actually attached to my heart! Enclosed ever so subtly that one would hardly have noticed had they not gone tugging on the other end of the string!

I begin to follow my string, wondering what adventure awaits me, and did everyone else have one just like me, or was it only I? How truly fascinating. I would have to table these conversations for another time, however, as right now, I am on my way out the door trailing this ever-expanding little red string.

My lovely red twinning is quite magical, I realise. As I walk forward, it grows longer, but when I want to go home or put it away (so to speak), the string simply disappears back inside my chest. Rolling and tumbling its way back to its home, until it is ready to be used again to lead the way.

* * *

Well, as adventures go, this was one of plenty. There were moments of laughter, joy, tears, anger, shame, and grief. You see, this was a long walk down memory lane as I followed my red string and the stories it told. Weaving in and out along the windy path of my history, a vision of photographs of memories like old slides flashing one after the other. Sometimes in black in white, other times in bright colours. Always with sound, music, and conversations from days gone by. It was beautiful and heartbreaking, reliving these moments. I clung to my little red string as I continued down this long path, and I couldn't help but wonder where it was leading me. After all, it must end somewhere, the other end belonging and anchoring itself to another object or person, just like me. After all, whatever would this be for otherwise?

I think deep down I knew that the other thing was you. That tugging feeling on the other end of my red string was my connection to you. That we were still, after all these years, in some bizarre parallel universe kind of way, still together. That what we had never truly ended. After all this time, I never stopped loving you, thinking about you, praying each day, and wishing you all the goodness in the world.

Perhaps, you felt the same way for me too. The universe seemed to cross our paths now and then in funny and dubious ways, and I tried earnestly to reach out and break the walls between us so we could reunite in person once more. Thus far, alas, this has not happened.

But now I have my little red string, and it is connected to my heart on one end and yours on the other, and that gives me hope. It gives me a reason to believe that maybe we will meet again one day, if only as friends. And I have this little red string filled with memories of you and I and the times we shared together. The times we laughed, danced, cried, yelled, and drove each other mad, and even if you never come back to me, I know I am one of the lucky ones to have loved and been loved by someone as remarkable as you.

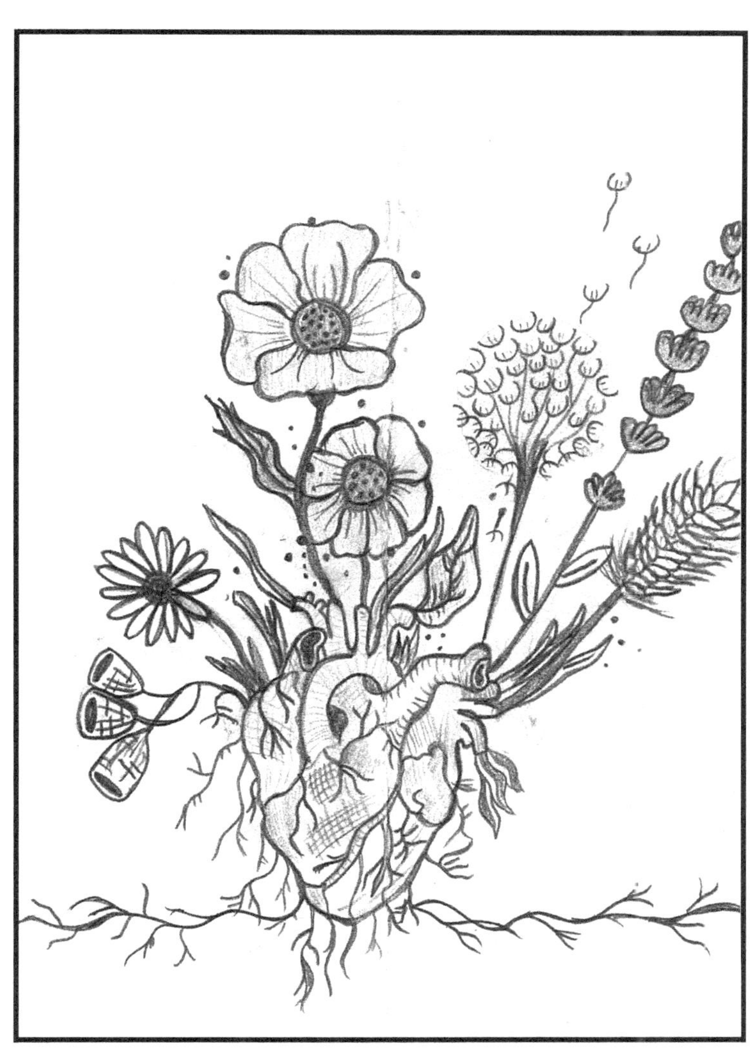

Anatomy Blooms

Look beyond the pines, behind the trees as far as your eyes can see. The skyline splashes across the treetops. All the colours of the sunset burst over the horizon, further than our arms can reach. Adventure waits; it's calling us home, whistling and howling on the wind like a familiar lullaby only an old close friend truly knows.

This is what we've been waiting for. To leave the darkness, debris, and chaos behind us like ashes. Instead, jump into the thousands of rays of sunshine of tomorrow. Start afresh. Anew.

This is our chance to begin again. Spread our wings and jump into the abyss. Let nature's wonders swallow us whole. Feel its beauty, its love, its sweet caress.

Close your eyes and leap.
Look beyond the pines, across the hilltops and sea coves, and fly, my friend. Our adventure awaits. Our lullaby is calling.

Soon we will be home.

I've looked for someone to love in all the wrong places
I've searched far and wide, round corners and various spaces.
Though I've talked with and met and even held hands with quite a few.
None of them come close to being my person, to being you.

No one understands me quite the way you used to.
I painted them a canvas of a thousand words, yet it was too few.
How I could move to music that wasn't even playing. How you and I spent dusk till dawn
dancing and swaying.

Or that I watch tv shows repeatedly and how it feels like home.
Parks and Rec and Gilmore Girls make me feel less alone.
And Harry Potter slows my heart rate and breathing down
to a steady rhythm that almost feels like you're still around.

It's not the same though, as when we watched them together.
Lying entangled, spooning peacefully, for what felt like forever.
Our hands entwined tightly as though we were in prayer.
Thanking God for the life He blessed me with.
With a love so rare.

I miss the way we danced and rambled up and down the pool.
We jammed, laughed, schemed, and broke every rule.
Exercising to soul train, making strangers laugh and smile.
Children looking on with awe and glee and engaging with us if only for a while.

Now I'm on my own with the tunes, and even though I still dance,

it's not the same, and I see people awkwardly steal a glance.

As the music echoes off the water, resonating my loneliness and the part of me that's

gone.

This loss is beyond immense.

I don't think I'll find what we shared ever again.

It was once in a lifetime love, and I was lucky it was with my best friend.

Though it pains me still to feel your absence each day

I am learning to live with it and find my own way.

I am content with my lot in life and the joys that I share.

Maybe we'll cross paths again. Maybe we won't. Either way, I love you and I will always

care.

Madame Phoenix

When everything is taken away from us, it's only then we truly know who we are and learn to be grateful for the things we do have. It changes us. There is this pressure inside us. We want to sing and dance and love and shout for everyone to hear.

After recovering from the initial diagnosis of Functional Neurological Disorder after the car accident, I was filled with immense joy and gratitude. I was bursting at the seams; I wanted to tell the world:

"I am grateful! I am happy I can walk again and be able to talk normally. I am thankful that I recognise familiar faces and remember my name and the names of those around me. I am over the moon that I am going home."

I want to shout my love for everyone in my life from the rooftops. Hear me when I tell you this, because I know this to be true as I have stared death in the face too many times before and thought of all the things I should have said and done.

When you love someone, don't waste a moment: tell them. Even if you're scared. Whether it's a friend, mum, dad, brother, sister, a mate at your local pub, or the one who holds that little red string to your heart—the one you love most of all. Tell them. Tell them all. Say what they mean to you. Don't hesitate with love. Say it out loud. Share it. Embrace it. Believe in it. Have faith and hope and give it freely without fear or expectations. Love unconditionally. The world is better for it. YOU will be better for it. So, go on, what are you waiting for? Tell the people in your life today, now, what they mean to you and how much you love them.

Oh my! How lucky are we? Look at that bee!

What a privilege to be surrounded by such beauty!

To see flowers bloom and the mighty birds soar,

Their wings on which nature's secret roars,

Up in the air acting like they don't care,

But they do and they sure have flare.

Watch them as they fly, showing folks like you and I,

The tide grows stronger whilst the trees multiply.

Our animals, they may be struggling, but they're holding steady.

Even the wombats accommodated the homeless during the black summer of 2020.

Our world is dying; there is no question or any doubt.

However, remember the power of wildlife, how it never backs down from a fight.

Its resilience is written over thousands of years of human history.

Overcoming obstacles and making paths that have led to environmental victories.

Even now scientists are discovering new creatures never heard or seen before.

So, isn't that something to be grateful for as well as worth fighting for?

Take your triple R action – REDUCE, REUSE & RECYCLE – and join the stance against
climate change.

Start with something simple like recycling cans or shifting to free range.

Be the change you want to see in this universe.

If we don't play our part soon enough, we shall all end up in one big hearse!

I believe in the greater good.

I believe that no matter how bad or evil some people are, there will always be that little

bit of good left in them. That ounce of decency that still lives deep down inside of them.

I believe that we are all equal.

I believe we have no right to judge another – no matter how good or bad you are, and how good or bad they are.

I believe that if you truly love someone you would do anything for them, and no matter how hard you try you can never forget someone you love.

I believe that goodbye is the saddest word you'll ever say and the hardest heartbreak you'll ever feel.

I believe it is better to be hated for who you are than loved for who you are not.

I believe you should always try to tell the truth, even when it hurts.

I believe in breaking down, in being emotional, letting go.

I believe in trying your best, and that it's okay if you don't always succeed, because we learn more from mistakes than we do our successes.

I believe there are two sides to every story.

I believe in giving without expecting anything in return. Loving – unconditionally.

I believe that even though I can say I love you to hundreds of people, I can't always say it to myself – and maybe you feel the same way.

I believe that the strong are not those who do not fall but rather those who can pick themselves up after they have fallen. Even when everything and everyone around them are breaking apart at the seams.

I believe in hope and faith.

I believe God is always listening, even when we don't say a word.

I believe in being free. In dancing, singing, screaming, loving, crying, thinking, and feeling.

I believe in being affectionate and intimate. Don't be afraid to hold someone's hand, hug them, or kiss them. Physical contact is so powerful.

I believe in losing control.

I believe in art and its power to nurture the soul.

I believe that music is one of the reasons I wake up in the morning.

Most of all, I believe in relationships and human connection. At the end of the day, it's the people you love that matter the most. Above all else – education, money, fame, reputation, status – none of these things really matter. The love we share and the connections we make are truly what hold us together. So, find your tribe and don't let go, because you need them and they need you, and that's just the way life is. What are you waiting for?

Drowning

> I struggled under the weight of all the hardship and pressure.
> Everything I held dear was disappearing. Slipping from my fingers and
> vanishing, never to be seen again, like sunken treasure.

Sinking

> I crumbled beneath the weight; my body sank to the ocean floor.
> It was empty, dark, and cold.
> I curled into a ball.
> I couldn't take it anymore.

Resurfacing

> But suddenly, a light appeared, shining through.
> The more I wrote and drew, this light, it grew and grew,
> and soon I started to rise.
> Resurfacing at last, after such a dark demise.

Floundering

> Struggling still, I floundered about;
> the obstacles I faced with determination and strong will.

Treading water

> Soon I found my rhythm, the words I wrote were music etched deep
> within my soul that I could dance to.
> The artwork I sketched was my heartbreak and trauma, which I could
> work through.

Swimming, Gazing

> I lay on my back, smiling as the sun kissed my cheeks, and the ocean
> lapped at my thighs.
> I turned my head from the shoreline back to the sunshine and blue
> skies.
> Tears rolled down my face as I gently whispered to myself,
> "You did it. You survived."

ACKNOWLEDGMENTS

Firstly, to my immediate family: Mum, Dad, Kellie, Daniel, Bradley, and my two nephews Marshall and Hayden. Thank you for walking this journey with me, particularly in the early stages. Our family's support and love were a huge contributor to my recovery. In particular, Marshall (Bear) and (Chook) who bring me such immense joy and light even on the darkest of days. You are both, my knights in shining armour and together we will continue to slay dragons, defeat giants fight for truth, justice and equality in our days to come. Secondly, to my Banshee family. You saw, perhaps more than anyone, how debilitating and traumatising this condition was for me in the early stages before I went into rehab. You also understood how hard it was for me to walk away from my career working with children, of how much they meant to me, and the loss I felt as a result. Thank you for always giving me a shoulder to cry on and making me laugh even at the worst of times. Special thanks to Ken and Nina Weaver who were always there for me and allowed me to grieve in my own way at my own pace what I had loss and how my life changed. I will never forget that. To the wonderful FND community, who are always there for support, guidance, and a vent! The power of your understanding and empathy as individuals who also suffer from this awful condition and can offer firsthand experience advice does not go unnoticed. I would not have survived the early stages of diagnosis without your assistance; you were my lifeline in the storm. In memory and gratitude of Mick, who always believed in me and told me, "You just keep being you, the Phoenix, because you're going places and you're going to make it someday, and there's nobody quite like you." Joan Baker, my GP, my friend, my fellow spiritual ally, and confidant. Thank you for always believing in me, even when the rest of the medical field said there was nothing wrong. Thank you for always making me feel heard and seen. I am incredibly blessed to have you in my life. And finally, to my two best friends, Jade Demnar and Sarah Gavranich without whom I would not be the person I am today, nor would I be standing as strong and tall as I am now. Your devotion, love, and support are truly appreciated. I have won the lottery with you two by my side. Here's to another 20+ years friendship.